DESIGN EDUCATION: a vision for the future

DESIGN EDUCATION: a vision for the future

Edited by Ken Baynes and Eddie Norman

Published by: Loughborough Design Press Ltd, 16 Wightman Close, Shepshed, Leicestershire, LE12 9NQ

Copyright for this edition © 2013, Loughborough Design Press

For information on all Loughborough Design Press publications, please visit our website: www.ldpress.co.uk

Printed by Printondemand-worldwide.com, UK
The paperback is FSC and PEFC certified

ISBN: [paperback] 978-1-909671-03-4
eISBN: [ePub] 978-1-909671-04-1
eISBN: [mobi] 978-1-909671-05-8

PEFC Certified

This product is
from sustainably
managed forests
and controlled
sources

www.pefc.org

PEFC™
PEFC/16-33-415

Mixed Sources

Product group from well-managed
forests, and other controlled sources
www.fsc.org Cert no. TT-COC-002641
© 1996 Forest Stewardship Council

FSC

ACKNOWLEDGEMENTS

We would like to thank the Design and Technology Association for permission to update and reproduce the 2010 John Eggleston Memorial Lecture given by Ken Baynes and most importantly, the contributors to this book who were able to make space in their diaries to respond to our call at very short notice. The urgency was forced upon us and we are very grateful for the high quality of the responses made despite the time constraints.

Book and cover design: Eddie Norman

DESIGN EDUCATION: a vision for the future

WHY THIS BOOK?

For now ...

This short book is intended as an angry, but measured response to the Government's new National Curriculum proposals for Design and Technology and Art and Design in England. However its scope is much wider than national or 'subject' boundaries, as it is written from the standpoint of Design Education.

The new curriculum proposals are frankly astonishing. They are a tired re-hash of old-fashioned approaches and ideas. How such a document came to be written is hard to understand but the result is not recognizable either as current good practice, or as the views of any of the organizations who might have been consulted for informed and authoritative proposals.

There is little to be gained by Loughborough Design Press joining in the chorus of criticism that will certainly be directed at this folly. We support the criticism of course, but also believe the time has come to put forward a more relevant vision of the future. Consequently:

- Christopher Frayiing has written a Foreword analysing the recent history that has led to the current position.
- The Editors - Ken Baynes and Eddie Norman - have put forward their recommendations in the form of a letter.
- Phil Roberts has described the characteristics of design education and provided a means to review and develop design curricular provision and practice in general education.
- Eddie Norman has provided an overview of the research foundations for design education that have been constructed by colleagues over the last decades.

For the future ...

We believe that at a point in the not too distant future, even politicians will recognize the vital importance of design education. We have decided, therefore, to publish this specially commissioned and rapidly produced book. It is structured round the 2010 John Eggleston Memorial Lecture given by Ken Baynes at the Design and Technology Association Education and International Research Conference at Keele University. The lecture was entitled 'Models of Change: The future of design education'.

The lecture proposed seven key themes around which a future vision of design education could be framed:

1 The aims of design education
2 The significance of practical education
3   Encouraging the imagination
4 The cognitive value of aesthetic awareness
5 The value of learning through making
6 The creative relationships between designing and making
7 The educational purpose of doing design projects

We have invited leading academics in the design education field to develop the discussion further. Each has taken one of Ken Baynes' themes as a starting point. The aim is to identify the Agenda for a future review of design education policy that could lead eventually to a curriculum and related teaching strategies fit for the 21st Century. Ken Baynes has revised and extended his lecture to cover some of the social and cultural issues at stake and also act as introductions to each of the seven thematic contributions.

We intend this book to be read by politicians, manufacturers, business people, school governors, headteachers, interested parents, policy makers and other stakeholders. Most of all it is directed at teachers in those curriculum areas related to design education. We hope to give them a new sense of self-confidence in themselves and in the value of the ideas, knowledge and skills that they teach.

BOOK STRUCTURE

It is perhaps unusual for there to be an explanation of the structure of a book, but it seems essential on this occasion. This book is the result of contributions made freely by committed colleagues who believe in the future of design education. It is not a series of papers that have been analysed and which lead to particular recommendations presented in its concluding chapters. The recommendations are made by the Editors at the beginning of the book having read the papers but not consulted their colleagues. This was partly a result of the timescale within which this book was written, but also, and more significantly, because the papers that follow explore the rich agendas that a full understanding of design education must encompass. They are a starting point for future discussions, not papers for which the recommendations put forward here represent an endpoint.

How can we make the best use of subject traditions, skilled teachers and existing good practice? We need to revisit some knotty conceptual issues, attempt to sharpen our understanding of our aims, and engage with the fundamentals of design and designing.

The contributions developing the discussions surrounding the seven key themes move this agenda forward. It would be hoped that future curricular provision that took these issues into account would result in credible proposals for the future of design education.

Taken together these contributions provide both the key theoretical positions and practical resources to enable the development of design education curricula fit for the 21st century.

CONTENTS

For now ...

FOREWORD   8
Christopher Frayling

RECOMMENDATIONS   11
Ken Baynes and Eddie Norman

CHARACTERISTICS OF DESIGN EDUCATION: Reviewing and   13
developing design curricular provision and practice in
general education
Phil Roberts

DESIGN EDUCATION RESEARCH   20
Eddie Norman

For the future ...

THE EMPTY SPACE: Seven Key Themes   25
Ken Baynes

    1. The Aims of Design Education   34
    Phil Roberts

    2. The Significance of Practical Education   42
    Eddie Norman & Ken Baynes

    3. Encouraging the Imagination   52
    Stephanie Atkinson

    4. The Cognitive Value of Aesthetic Awareness   61
    Krysia Brochocka & Ken Baynes

    5. The Value of Learning through Making   69
    Gill Hope

    6. The Creative Relationships between Designing and Making   78
    Niall Seery & Eddie Norman

    7. The Educational Purpose of Doing Design Projects   87
    Eileen Adams

FINAL WORD   96
Ken Baynes

REFERENCES   97

AUTHOR PROFILES   105

FOREWORD

In 1988, when the Educational Reform Act made Britain the first country in the world to introduce by law mandatory Design and Technology (D&T) exams for all 16 year olds, it looked as though the academic arguments - and the specialized research - about the benefits of D&T in secondary schools had at last been accepted by the establishment: arguments about design as an intellectual/practical subject in its own right, as a way of thinking about, and approaching, other academic subjects *and* as a source of rich vocational possibilities. D&T had, it seemed, shaken off its late Victorian associations with Mr Chippy in the woodwork room and with 'low-attaining' students who had trouble coping with words and numbers - shaken it off among teachers, learners, teacher-educators, school governors, politicians and interested parents. Design had achieved 'parity of esteem' with the other core disciplines – remember that phrase? – rather than being taught in the outhouse.

The focus of the argument might change - from 'problem-solving', 'critical evaluation' via 'learning through doing', 'the iterative process' to 'the creative industries' - and the discipline might seem to be in a constant state of self-clarification which to the uncharitable resembled navel-gazing - but this was from a position of well-earned confidence and strength. When, in the mid-1990s, just after the 'Design and Make' reforms to the curriculum, 'the creative industries' argument was added to the mix, it gave design extra visibility as a key driver of economic success. Granted, 'the creative industries' were at some level a rhetorical construct which didn't really exist as a collective - I mean, what do the fashion business, the software industry, the antiques trade and publishing *really* have in common? – but it was a very effective argument in its day. I was involved, in the early part of this century, as Chair of the Design Council and Rector of the Royal College of Art, in trying hard to establish design as the hyphen between Science, Technology and Engineering - the silent partner in STEM. And for a moment it looked as though this might actually happen: a senior government minister said to me that he thought it already had happened! Oh, and a well-researched report in the early 2000s concluded that D&T had the lowest truancy rate of all school subjects: it *engaged* young people in ways other subjects could only envy. The sort of statistic that politicians love.

And then the tide turned. Quite suddenly. 'The creative industries' dropped from public discourse, to make way for 'productive industry'. Design was not included among the 'priority subjects' in the Browne Review of Higher Education - a real disaster for art and design colleges and faculties. The Russell Group of universities announced that Art and D&T were no longer to be considered credible pre-requisites - not 'challenging' enough for entry into their high achieving institutions. Politicians of all persuasions reverted to talking about Design as a pre-apprenticeship subject, filed in the box 'vocational', about training rather than education. They seemed to forget William Morris' celebrated observation that training was something you did with dogs. They did sometimes wax nostalgic about a magic moment in the craft workshop. Then there was the dark night of the English Baccalaureate, which always reminded me of discussions in the Design Research Unit at the RCA about whether the three Rs should *really* be 'reading, wroughting/wrighting, rithmetic', for which there was actually some historical evidence. It had looked at the turn of this century as though the message about design in schools had been thoroughly received and understood - and yet it clearly had not. What went wrong?

Some have argued that Design tried too hard to be all things to all people - raising expectations the discipline could not possibly deliver. That having been confined to woodworking, metalworking and weaving for so many years, it got into the dangerous habit of over-justifying itself: a recipe for disappointment. Others have argued that the very diversity of Design in and across the curriculum led to all sorts of muddles about where the *heart* of the subject lay (process, product, or impact), which in turn led to patchy teaching - at first because the Craft generation still dominated in classrooms, later because of the reaction 'when in doubt about simulated design projects, go formulaic' and treat the subject as linear, rigid, constrained. The Sorrell Foundation initiative JoinedUpDesignforSchools explicitly countered over-complicated projects where 'there is just too much work to do' in the time available, by foregrounding the client/design relationship in more realistic settings. Others still have argued that Design tended to remain physically isolated from the rest of the school, which did not help its supposed integral connections with other core disciplines: this was certainly my experience whenever I was asked to open a shiny new Design wing which conformed to all the latest, increasingly complex health and safety requirements. Out of sight, out of mind? Wearing my higher education hat, I also noticed that design students - if they went into school teaching - were much more likely to gravitate towards the art room than the design studio/workshop/space: they did not have the same respect for D&T, and its confusing academic claims, coming as they did from a learning environment where 'academic' was still a dirty word. Debates about whether Design had its disciplinary base in Art or Science seemed a very long way away.

Whatever the reasons - and they probably include all the above, and more besides - there is no doubt at all that Design in schools has lost ground, esteem and credibility in the early twenty-first century. In political discourse, there has been a strong swing away from Design as a core intellectual/social/academic pursuit: at its most extreme, this swing has taken the form of trying to put the clock back not just to Mr Chippy but to Mr Chips. The big arguments, which used to cut ice, have come to be seen as broken-backed: the claim that designerly thinking is valuable in <u>all</u> academic subjects seems to cancel out the more specific and pragmatic claim that design is central to economic/industrial development. Those of us who can remember the excitement, the sense of *promise*, surrounding design education in the years 1973-1995 - the visionary years, when we all talked animatedly of the experience of design in schools enabling learners to *make a difference* in the cultural world, and about savvy citizens in the modern hi-tech universe - are beginning to wonder whether our conclusions were ever *really* accepted, deep down, by the powers that be. Several of those pioneers have contributed to this volume. I've been around this debate for so long that a student once called me a 'designosaur'. As has often been noted, very few senior people in public life owe their elevated position to design education - even if they *do* sometimes get misty-eyed about the good old days making table-mats. I once made this point at a design conference in Hanover, and rashly asked the delegates if they could think of a single senior politician who had specialized during their youth in art or design. One hand went up. 'Well, we did try that once , in the 1930s'. I vowed never to use that line in Germany again.

It is time to re-group, re-consider, re-research, re-energise the debate, re-iterate, re-present ideas as widely as possible through a variety of media, re-form networks and form new ones, re-consider teaching and learning *to* design and *through* design, re-explore why design in schools seems such an awkward subject. Time to differentiate very carefully indeed between advocacy and research. Time to make teaching more attractive to those with a design background. Time to have the confidence not to over-claim. Look where that has led us. In short, time for a 'vision of the future'.

The trenchant, well-argued essays in this volume, written by some of the foremost thinkers and researchers about design education, are an excellent start. Design is far too important a subject to leave to the whims of political fashion. As William Morris once said, in answer to a question about design's significance after a lecture he had just given, 'design gives us hope'.

Professor Sir Christoper Frayling
March 2013

RECOMMENDATIONS

Ken Baynes and Eddie Norman

Although the subject matter of this letter is the specific content of the English National Curriculum proposals for Design and Technology and Art and Design, the crass nature of the Government's proposals should concern us all. We are in danger of destroying something uniquely excellent in our education system. It is not simply that Mr Gove's team have ignored leading figures in the design, engineering and media industries, employers organizations and specialist teachers' associations: it is also that they have completely failed to recognize the value of Britain's contribution to design education. This is one of the few curriculum areas where we are world-leading. Art and Design and Design and Technology provide creative energy in the curriculum, encourage young people to use their imaginations, consider the needs of others and look to the future.

Countries which have previously looked to us for curriculum models and inspiration in teaching and learning approaches to design, may in future look in amazement at official vandalism. They may express sympathy but they are more likely to find us a laughing stock. Certainly the English model of design education, which crosses the boundaries between art, design and technology, will no longer be providing a relevant curriculum model for the 21st Century.

However, beyond such a loss of face, and indeed, beyond the pragmatic arguments for the importance of design education and its contributions to economic well-being and the creative industries, there is potentially an even greater loss. There has been a growing understanding of Design as a third culture, one as significant as Science and the Humanities, which has its own epistemology and language. Such progress stems from the work of Bruce Archer and his colleagues within the Design Education Unit at the Royal College of Art in the 1970s and 1980s. It had been thought that decision-makers within the educational establishment had begun to share some of this understanding and recognize its importance for children's learning. Apparently, this has not been the case, and so it is important for our voice to be heard. In this sense, it is vital that the Government listens to us.

Is design a 'proper' subject? As academics we argue that it is. Design education is backed by coherent pedagogical theory and a substantial body of research. Over the past month we have 'plied our trade' and contributed to a book of recommendations and essays which is about to be published by Loughborough Design Press. The aim of this short book is to provide a launch pad for a future design education curriculum. We have also addressed the immediate situation and produced a freely downloadable paper available at www.ldpress.co.uk which summarizes the essential nature of design education, reviews relevant research and makes a number of recommendations.

That all this has been done in a very short period and on a non-profit basis by authors and publisher alike, is a measure of how seriously we take the Government's actions.

These are the recommendations. The Government should:

- Establish a new institution in higher education devoted to researching the theory, content and pedagogy of design education and offering courses for teachers. It would also work with existing institutions offering teacher training.

- Establish a 'Commission' with the task of developing a design education curriculum. It should be able to fund experiments and trials in schools.

- Adopt Professor Roberts' paper as an initial framework for the future development of design education.

- Recognize the research contributions that have been made towards the understanding of design education.

- Set up two or three 'research consortia' of schools (primary and secondary) who would attempt to achieve exemplary practice in design education.

- Re-establish a new body based on the 1970s confederation of organisations devoted to the development of design education. Teachers' professional bodies, designers' professional bodies, pressure groups etc. If they can be persuaded, it should be established under the auspices of the Royal Society of Arts.

- Organize a travelling national exhibition of exemplary design work from primary and secondary schools.

- Establish an authoritative body representing universities, business, the design professions and schools to draft new GCSE and A-level design examinations based on the submission and assessment of design projects backed with theoretical papers on technology, materials, aesthetics and design history and seek wide acceptance of the examination and its methods of assessment.

And, in the immediate future, whilst the effects of these actions are coming into play:

- Abandon the current proposals for reforming Design and Technology and Art and Design within the National Curriculum while acknowledging the national importance of design education as an element in both these subject areas.

- Listen to the advice it has received through, for example, the Design and Technology Association.

- Do nothing, or implement one of the credible proposals that have been developed during the consultation phase as an interim measure.

CHARACTERISTICS OF DESIGN EDUCATION: Reviewing and developing design curricular provision and practice in general education

Phil Roberts

1   The concept of *Design* encompasses a very wide range of everyday human experience, enterprise, and action – that is, not to just the disciplines and areas of professional design practice.   Within this, the concept of *designing* refers to taking purposeful action in and on the world.   Such action is intended to have effect: *viz*, to bring about some kind of *change in the world*.   It can also, obviously enough, have unintended consequences as well as those which are intended; not all design activity – consciously intended or otherwise - is necessarily or inevitably 'good' in its outcomes or its 'added value'.   In the context of general education, *design-educational activity* is primarily intended to bring about some *change in the learner*: that is, in capability, in knowledge, in understanding, or whatever. Thus, designing is essentially and at the highest level of generality to do with bringing about required or desirable change - in some aspect of the world, or in the agent of the activity, or in both.

Hence, the objects, functions, and outcomes of design-educational activity can be understood both as *a means* towards achieving some desired or required end (*eg*, the design and making of some tangible artefact, with the artefact as the required end) and as the moving towards an *educational end* (*eg*, enhanced design cognition).   At this point, we need to be aware of the risk of confusion illustrated, for instance, in a question such as: 'Are we to appraise the artefact or some aspect of the pupil's development?'   Complexity is no surprise though and, especially, because designing and learning display similar logics-in-use.

People are enabled to take part in designing through the possession and use of a distinctive capacity of mind: *viz*, for making images and models of the world - 'in the mind's eye' we say – as it is and as it might be. The capacity for engaging in *cognitive modelling* is essential to the practice of design activity, to designing-learning, to apprehending the phenomena of Design, and to manipulating aspects of experience and future visions.   It follows that the fundamental objectives of any design-educational curriculum include the development of the capacity for cognitive modelling, along with the capacities for addressing real-world states-of-affairs. The latter, being problematised for pedagogic purposes, are in principle boundless and, even when brought to a sufficient 'definition' within curricular activities, are therefore not to be confined within school-subject boundaries.

2   The phenomena of Design, real-world states-of-affairs, curriculum subjects, and the activities of designing-as-learning can collectively be referred to as the *design dimension* of the school's entire formal (and informal) curriculum.   If Design is thought of as a broad *field* or as a broad *dimension* of a school's curriculum, it also has recognisable *areas* (including, as examples, communication design, graphic

design, product design, textiles/fashion, design & technology, environmental studies, etc). Experience in such areas is offered, in general education, through the provision of *school curriculum subjects*, most obviously in the secondary age-range of general education although the 'informal curriculum' is significant too. Design activity is evident, then, across and beyond the curriculum.

3   In a mature educational world, teachers themselves would be responsible for, and would lead, the development of educational practice. They would identify and continuously refresh their subject matters, and their teaching & learning.

And, indeed, deliberate and effective teacher-led attention to design as a dimension of the curriculum can of course be found; and exemplars of design-related subject-based practices and curriculum activities are not rare. What is interesting is how some practitioners retain the freshness in their teaching and learning, and how such a quality of teaching and learning might be institutionalised.

In reality though, any headteacher can embody and enact an approach via his or her oversight of a school's curriculum; any head of department can; a lone teacher (specialist or not), can also ensure and provide the conditions for significant teaching and learning.

What follows is one approach towards achieving a continuously lively design education, but one which is no more than one instrument of many possible instruments and approaches. There are other voices, other instruments, other points of view. Its principles need to be considered and used in a 'loose-fit' way: it's certainly not something to be adopted in a simplistic check-list approach: that, ironically, would be precisely against its spirit and intention, and be counter-productive. The check-list approach – or, more precisely, using uncritically the check-lists of others - is rarely effective in ensuring quality. Not all the questions may be considered pertinent; and others might be devised that are considered to be more useful to particular circumstances. Some modification would doubtless be especially appropriate when considering the primary school age-range curriculum. The strong view, of course, is that which regards all check-lists with scepticism and, also, that teachers should be fully responsible for devising, in a principled way, their own curricular and course contents, and their own curriculum review processes. So, with those caveats in mind, we need to proceed in as generous a spirit as possible of 'trying it for size' and being willing to use it as possibly no more than a starting point in our own institutional circumstances. And, of course, we would need to be alert to providing the substantiating evidence that would support our responses.

4 A review and development schedule (for want of a better term: the focus is to do with the processes of appraisal)

Generally:

- Does the school/department/section ensure the particular or unique contribution of [*here the user should insert the name of whichever school subject(s) he or she wishes to consider – Design, Art, Art & Design, D&T, IT, Textiles, Environmental Studies …*] to children's learning and reflection upon their experience?
- Does the school's curriculum and its timetable organisation enable cooperative learning and collaborative teaching between subject-based departments?
- By what means and in what range of activities are pupils enabled to reflect on their experience, and to make images and artefacts which explore or express something of their experience?
- By what means and in what range of activities (and school subjects) are pupils enabled to express and communicate aspects of personal identity, value, and meaning?
- What kinds of activities do pupils engage in which will enable them to identify and respond personally to the qualities and character of the visual communications, products, and surroundings that make up the natural and man-made world (beginning with the school)?
- Do pupils use media and forms appropriate to their intentions, 'audiences', and subject matter?
- Do the pupils have access to, and use, a range of tools and materials to increase awareness of their functional, technical, and aesthetic potential?

With regard to the development of historical and cultural awareness:

- What activities enable pupils to identify, express and respond personally to the social, economic, technological, and aesthetic factors and values which underlie the historical development of the made world (and which are displayed in a variety of cultures)?
- How are pupils enabled to recognise and respect cultural diversity and the cultural values underlying the surface appearance of visual communications, products, and places?
- Does the [*here, insert particular subject title as appropriate*] programme reflect a balance between well-established, developing, and new technologies?
- Are [*here, insert particular subject title as appropriate*] activities biased (in whatever direction) with regard to their cultural framework? Are [*insert particular subject title*] activities biased (in whichever direction) with regard to gender?
- Are pupils enabled to use a number of the analytical methods developed by historians and critics in understanding their own work and the design activity of others?

15

With regard to the development of abilities to think, to image 'in the mind's eye', to plan, design, invent, and produce:

- What kinds of activities, and what range, give pupils experience of identifying their, and others', needs, wants, and visions of the future that can best or only be explored through [*here, insert particular subject title, kinds of activity, or whatever*]?
- Do the activities extend from those which are inwardly motivated to those which are externally stimulated?
- Do pupils use, and make transformations between, two- and three-dimensional forms and media, language, and notational systems and do they have access to information technologies?
- Do design [*and other*] assignments, tasks, and projects give pupils experience of making significant decisions?
- Of choosing against criteria (theirs and others')?
- Of recognising and accepting the potential and actual consequences of their actions/designed outcomes?
- Of recognising different points of view?
- Do assignments, tasks, and project-based activities give experience of 'defining' (or articulating sufficiently), analysing, and resolving (rather than necessarily solving) problems (or states-of-affairs) in the areas of visual communication, product, and environmental design?

With regard to the development of critical skills in [*here, insert particular subject title as may be required*]:

- Do assignments enable pupils to analyse their own work together with a characteristic range of others' design work?
- Do they experience different role views?
- Are pupils enabled to discuss in writing, words and images, and from a variety of viewpoints, the feelings, motivations, values and achievements exhibited in their own and others' work?
- Does such discussion include the work of artists, craftspeople, and a range of specialist professional designers?
- Are pupils enabled to evaluate the functional, visual, economic, and social consequences of their own and others' decisions?
- Are pupils enabled to define, explain, and justify – using appropriate media – a personal stance in relation to their own and others' design work?

With regard to the scope and extent of the design curriculum: breadth, balance, relevance, and differentiation:

Breadth and Balance

- How wide a range of skills, techniques, media, technologies does each pupil experience?
- Is there a considered balance between work in two- and three-dimensional forms?
- Is a range of tools, materials, and technologies accessible to and used by all pupils?
- Specific to Art [or to Art & Design], is experience balanced between the Fine Arts & Crafts strand and, on the other complementary hand, the more-applied design strand of Art & Design?
- Is there a balance in the pupils' experience with regard to the roles of artist, craftsperson, designer, maker, user, critic, citizen?
- Does the work give pupils a balanced experience with regard to visual communication, product design, and environmental design?

Relevance

- Does the work (whether to do with exploring and expressing matters of identity, value, and meaning, or with more-applied designerly activities) derive from and relate to pupils' lived experience, aspirations, and visions of the future and their own futures?
- How do activities and subject matter relate to the pupils' developing biographies (including possible career aspirations)?
- What criteria of 'relevance' do the staff use?
- Do pupils or staff or both determine 'relevance'?
- If there is disagreement about 'relevance', on what basis are decisions made?

Differentiation

- To what extent do assignments, projects and activities take account of differences of abilities and dispositions of pupils?
- Is the subject matter likely to have similar appeal to girls and boys? Does it matter?
- Is differentiation in subject matter made which takes account of possible gender-cultural interests and concerns?
- Are assignments, worksheets, teaching aids, resources, and 'design briefs' pitched at a number of different levels of complexity and difficulty?
- Is there group work and project-based work which enables pupils of (currently) different abilities to learn from each other?
- Is there a considered balance between individual and group work?
- Are tasks, exercises, and assignments set that have specific learning objectives?

With regard to learning and teaching beyond that provided by a single department:

- Does the design work enable or require access to other departments?
- Does the school's curriculum and timetable organisation facilitate or hinder this?
- Is there co-operative learning and teaching between departments, informally or formally?
- Are there discussions with teachers in other departments/sections to consider whether certain content might be taught, or competencies developed, through co-operative approaches to teaching and learning?
- Are there aspects of an activity or of subject matter which might better be taught and learned by using collaborative approaches and arrangements?
- Are other teachers invited to see pupils' work and to hear the educational objectives of design activity, and to see pupils at work?
- Is comment, advice, and criticism invited?

With regard to the design curriculum: issues of curricular progression and continuity, and the assessment of pupils' development:

- What account is taken of pupils' curricular design activities and experience gained in earlier schools?
- How refined a notion of progression and of 'necessary' sequence is possible or justifiable?
- Do these include reference to, for example, the notion of the 'spiral curriculum'?
- How does (any) one activity, assignment or project stand in relation to others?
- How do curricular activities relate to the different 'stages' of the pupils' personal and cognitive development?
- Does subject matter, or do objectives, emphases, or organisation of teaching and learning, change relative to the school's age range; the pupils' age group; the stages of pupils' development?
- What criteria are used in the assessing of pupils' learning-through-designing?
- Do these criteria distinguish between *means* and *educational ends* when considering any artefacts that are made? (Or, between process, tangible artefact, and cognitive or other achievement?)
- Are the essential educational natures, purposes and objectives of design activity similar wherever they are practised, or are there significant and defensible differences of emphasis and intention according to context (*viz*, the primary school, the 11-16 secondary school, post-16 provision in general education, Further Education vocational provision, Higher Education provision, the design studio/workshop)?

5 Some concluding comments

Any teacher reviewing and appraising curricular provision in the design curricular dimension of general education might be well advised to be alert to some conceptual pitfalls which lie in wait. Some of these conceptual distinctions have been offered in this paper: *viz*, between design as a general *field* of human experience and activity; as a *field* of professional disciplines with *disciplinary areas;* as a *dimension* (of the schools' curriculum) with some *school subjects* having an especially significant contribution to make. Then, it's useful to be alert to the dangers of using the word *design* as both verb and noun and, particularly, of using design as an abstraction which has the power to do things (as in, for instance, 'Design adds value', which is almost meaningless and certainly does nothing to help understanding: it is human activity – *designing* - which may, or may not, add value). Thus, useful distinctions can be observed between *design* and *designing:* they are not synonymous.

Similarly, there are careful distinctions to be observed between design educational activity, professional design activity, and non-professional design activity.

As it happens, it is similarly the case with the concept of *technology* and its usage. The concept refers, first, to the general relations between human purpose, materials, energy, and activity. But it is often used, secondly, and somewhat confusingly and not helpfully, as though it were a verb, and as though it were or could be an agent of action. Finally, it is frequently used without any distinction between the high-level of generality and the lower-level of specificity with the result that the particular is offered as though it were the general case. (Hence, *technology* – a non-specific concept - is frequently confused with some particular technology, *eg*, electronics technology.)

All this is to stress the need to be as precise as possible; the critic might see it as 'mere' pedantry. In reality however, the more precise use of language and the more precise usage of concepts matter because they affect, and effect, the general understanding and, more to the point in the world of action and of education, they affect fundamentally the nature and quality of education and of action in and on the world. The language of discourse and the meta-language of design matter.

One final iteration with which to conclude. A person can be engaged in designing, and in technologically-based activity, in the fullest sense, without there being any necessity to produce an artefact. That is, there is a transitive mode of designing which is as good an exemplar as the more commonly accepted instance which is exemplified in the designing and production of things (or artefacts). The design and production of things is a particular case of designing, not the general case. Designing can be characterised, at a high-level of generality, as being to do with *change* or, better, with *changing*: change in the agent of the activity and change brought about through the activity. Artefacts are means, not ends; the required ends consist in change.

DESIGN EDUCATION RESEARCH

Eddie Norman

Design education research is not a new area of activity, and there is a plausible case for considering its origins in the work of Pestalozzi (1746-1827), Fröbel (1781-1852), Cygnaeus (1810-1888) and Salomon (1849-1907), who developed the Sloyd approach (see Ólafsson and Thorsteinsson, 2009). As Table 1 indicates, research contributions concerning design in general education are well documented back to around 1970. The Table has been updated from Norman et al (2009), and paints a picture. The author is grateful to colleagues for their comments and suggestions relating to this table, but of course accepts full responsibility for any errors or omissions. However, it is clear that the last two decades have seen much activity as colleagues have sought to support the emerging practice relating to Design and Technology in general education.

The online hub, www.dater.org.uk, was established in 2008 to provide a central access point to the archives of research outputs (estimated number of outputs in brackets) from *IDATER (397), D&T Association International Research Conferences (178), NADE (National Association for Design Education) journals (90), Orange Series publications (11)* and *Design and Technology Education: an international journal (195)* and its predecessors *(1158)*. The hub facilitates a simultaneous online search of over 2000 research outputs. These are all open access, so that all teachers have access in support of practitioner research. The origins of these research outputs are highlighted in Table 1, and it can be observed that there are many other important sources that do not feature on the online hub eg the *PATT* and *CRIPT* conferences and academic journals such as the *International Journal of Technology and Design Education, The Journal of Technology Studies* and *The Journal of Technology Education*.

There will be debates about the rigour of the quality control procedures associated with some of these research outputs, but nearly all were peer reviewed. Hence academic colleagues at the time of their publication believed that they were worthy of publication.

The essential difficulty with reviewing design education research is its breadth and one way of considering contributions is through 3 categories.

- The designer(s): the individual(s) their capabilities and their competences for designing.
- The design context: the analysis of the knowledge, skills and values that they might possess.
- The interface: tools for designing and organisational structures that enhance designer's capabilities, competences and access to their context.

The derivation of these categories and their use in the analysis of the nature of effective contributions to design education research can be found in Norman (2011). The conclusions of this paper were that the characteristics of effective research in design education, perhaps unsurprising, paralleled those of the 'design research'strategy proposed by van den Akker *et al* (2006) for researchers in general education.

> '… design research may be characterised as:
> - Interventionist: the research aims at designing an intervention in the real world;
> - Iterative: the research incorporates a cyclic approach of design, evaluation, and revision;
> - Process orientated: a black box model of input-output measurement is avoided, the focus is on understanding and improving interventions;
> - Utility orientated: the merit of a design is measured, in part, by its practicality for users in real contexts; and
> - Theory orientated: the design is (at least partly) based upon theoretical propositions, and field testing of the design contributes to theory building'.
>
> (van den Akker *et al*, 2006: 5)

Many such contributions have been made over recent decades, and they have not been given the weight that they might have been in determining future curriculum policies.

TABLE 1 KEY RESEARCH EVENTS 1968-2009 SURROUNDING THE EMERGENCE OF DESIGN AND TECHNOLOGY IN ENGLAND

Year	Research events
1967	• *Project Technology* started at Loughborough College of Education (ended 1972)
1967	• *The Keele Project: Design and Craft Education* started (ended 1973)
1968	• *Studies in Design Education and Craft* (later *Studies in Design Education, Craft and Technology*) launched
1969	• *Art and Craft Education 8-13* project started at Goldsmiths' College (ended 1972)
1974	• *Design in General Education* project started at the Royal College of Art (ended 1975)
1973	• *International Perspectives of Design Education Conference,* University of Keele
1980	• Keith-Lucas report on *Design Education at Secondary Level* published by the Design Council
1982	• *Understanding Design and Technology* report by the Assessment of Performance Unit published
1984	• Graded Assessment Project - Kings College and ILEA: GAME, GAML, GACDT. Origin of 10 National Curriculum levels
1985	• First *Pupils Attitudes to Technology Conference (PATT)* • *APU D&T Project National Survey launched (1985 – 1990)*

1988	•	*1st DATER (Design and Technology Educational Research and Curriculum Development)* Conference at Loughborough University. One of a series of annual conferences.
	•	*Best of Studies in Design Education, Craft and Technology* published
1989	•	*Studies in Design Education, Craft and Technology* relaunched as *Design and Technology Teaching: a journal of new approaches*
	•	*The Journal of Technology Education* is launched by the ITEA
1990	•	TERU (the Technology Education Research Unit) was founded at Goldsmiths, University of London
1991	•	Final APU Report of *The Assessment of Performance in Design and Technology* published
	•	*The International Journal of Technology and Design Education* is published by Trentham Books
1992	•	*DATER* relaunched as an international conference *IDATER*
	•	*Teaching Design and Technology* published
	•	Loughborough University's *Orange Series* of publications is launched
	•	*1st PATT* Conference held in association with the ITEA
	•	Journal of the National Association for Design Education launched (… published until 2002)
	•	*INCOTE* (International Conference on Technology Education) Weimar, Germany
1994	•	Nuffield Project, RCA Schools Technology Project and TEP launched
1996	•	*Design and Technology Teaching: a journal of new approaches* is relaunched as *The Journal of Design and Technology Education*
	•	*Understanding Practice in Design and Technology* published
	•	*JISTEC* (Jerusalem International Science and Technology Education Conference)
1997	•	Publication of *The International Journal of Technology and Design Education* transfers to Kluwer
	•	*1st CRIPT (Centre for Research in Primary Technology)* conference at Birmingham City University (formally the University of Central England). The first of a series of biennial conferences
	•	*1st TENZ (Technology Education New Zealand) Conference*
	•	*Assessing Technology* published
2000	•	*Design and Technology International Millennium Conference* in London
	•	Publication of *Teaching and Learning Design and Technology: a guide to recent research and its applications*
	•	Engineering Council publications launched I*nteraction: the Relationship between Science and Design and Technology in the Secondary School Curriculum* (2000), *Design and Technology in a Knowledge Economy* (2001) *The Continuum of Design Education for Engineering* (2001)
	•	*WOCATE conference in Braunschweig, Germany*
	•	*1st Biennial Technology Education Research Conference* in Australia organised by Griffith University. The first of a series of biennial conferences.

2001	• 14th and final *IDATER* conference at Loughborough University
2002	• *1st Design and Technology Association Education and International Research Conference.* The first of a series of annual conferences
2003	• Publication of *Designs on the Curriculum? A review of literature on the impact of design and technology in schools in England* • Strategy Group Report *The Unique Contribution of Design and Technology* published
2004	• Loughborough's Design Education Research Group and the D&T Association jointly publish *Designerly Activity and Higher Degrees* (2004), *A Framework for Design and Design Education* (2005) and *Design and Democracy* (2005)
2005	• *The Journal of Design and Technology Education* is relaunched as *Design and Technology Education: an international journal* • *PATT-15*, the 20th Anniversary Conference was held in Haarlem leading to the publication of the first of a series by Sense Publishers: *International Handbook of Technology Education* • Project *e-scape* was founded at TERU
2006	• *Defining Technological Literacy: Towards an epistemological framework* published by Palgrave
2007	• *Researching Design Learning: Issues and findings from two decades of research and development* published by Springer • *Analysing Best Practices in Technology Education* published by Sense • First *IDATER Online* conference proceedings published *E-learning in Science and Design and Technology* • *Design & Technology – For the Next Generation* published by Cliffeco
2008	• *Researching Technology Education* and *The Cultural Transmission of Artefacts, Skills and Knowledge* published by Sense • The Online Hub www.dater.org.uk is launched and action research poster distributed to schools by D&T Association • New MA in Design Education launched by Goldsmiths
2009	• Launch of Loughborough University's 'Modelling' seminars and associated Orange Series publications • Launch of the DRS DESIG • *International Handbook of Research and Development in Technology Education* and *Project-based Learning: an Integrated Science, Technology, Engineering, and Mathematics (STEM) Approach* published by Sense
2010	• Design education strand included in the DRS Conference in Montreal • *Teaching & Learning Technology* conference held in Vancouver • Technology Education Research Group (TERG) formed at the University of Limerick • IDATER Online Conference on *Graphicacy and Modelling* at the University of Limerick

2011	• 1st Cumulus/DRS Symposium in Paris
	• Design education strand included in the IASDR Conference in Delft
	• *Positioning Technology Education in the Curriculum, Fostering Human Development Through Engineering and Technology Education* and *International Handbook of Primary Technology Education* published by Sense
2012	• DRS Conference in Bangkok results in a Special edition of *Design and Technology Education: an international journal*
	• *Technology Education for Teachers* published by Sense
2013	• *Design: Models of Change* and *Design Education: Visions for the Future* published by Loughborough Design Press
	• 2nd Cumulus/DRS Symposium in Oslo to result in a Special edition of *Design and Technology Education: an international journal*

The thousands of research contributions that have been made relating to design education demonstrate the commitment of teachers to evidence-based practice as the majority of them are founded on practitioners' research. They provide rather more than a starting point for curriculum planning, but it would appear that policymakers do not yet see their value. It is important that the messages embedded in these research contributions are made both evident and visible, so that, if they are ignored, the foolishness of the policymakers is also evident and visible

THE EMPTY SPACE: Seven Key Themes

Ken Baynes

The British education systems have an empty space where design education should be. In spite of declarations to the contrary, successive Government 'reforms' have resulted in schooling dominated by heritage (learning about the past), knowledge (learning things already known) and specific skills (learning known techniques). All these are valuable in themselves, but they are not sufficient, particularly in the rapidly-changing, highly competitive world of the 21st Century. They deal with the past and the present but not with the future. A part of the curriculum needs to be forward-facing, equipping children with the approaches and attitudes they will need to take on the role of shaping the future. Design, in conjunction with technology and the arts could be re-invented to fill this space.

Governments all over the world have grasped the idea that knowledge is essential for 'success' which, being translated means 'growth'. Knowledge is essential, of course. But if this knowledge cannot be applied to the extraordinarily important work of imagining alternative futures it will not deliver the goods and may well lead to unforeseen catastrophic results. Concepts of growth need moderating by a clear vision of ALL the possible repercussions. At the same time, vision, imagination, creativity and practical skills in making and management will be essential to the emergence of a viable, satisfying lifestyle.

Design occupies a key position because it is concerned with the future. The whole point of design activity is to bring new 'somethings' into being.

The emphasis must be on the imagination and how it can be encouraged in schools. Few can doubt that children HAVE imagination. Part of the problem is to prevent it being swamped by an apparently utilitarian curriculum. In fact, it would be very utilitarian indeed to foster young people's imaginations. It Is exactly what society and the environment need.

The mental processes involved in design activity and appreciating design are now well understood. Since the 1970s neuroscience and studies of human development have substantiated the intuitive proposals of earlier researchers. It is now quite clear that design activity results from the ability of the human mind to construct causal models of the world and to use those models to imagine changes to the world. That is in the mind. This mental activity is mirrored and extended by externalized models – drawings, prototypes, computer programs. They 'make visible' the thoughts and proposals about the future and enable others to share and eventually (sometimes) to act together to bring the proposals into reality. The externalized models also enable their originator to see them in a new light, to manipulate and to change them. It is one of the most important of human activities. It is how, for better or worse, the human species has come to dominate the planet.

Design education has assumed more and more importance as technology and industrialization have provided the means for rapid change. For centuries before the Enlightenment and the Industrial Revolution, practical skills (including design) were learnt in the home or 'on the job'. This did not mean that design lacked any theoretical or epistemological grounding. Theory, mainly to do with technique, technology, aesthetics and making skills goes back thousands of years and can be found in many different cultures. The existence of 'sufficient' theory is evident in the extraordinary monuments, water engineering, palaces, temples and weapons that exist from the past. There were also specifically theoretical works. The Roman engineer/architect Vitruvius wrote *De Architectura*, one of the first handbooks intended for the education of future professionals. It includes sections on modelling and aesthetics as well as mathematics, building techniques and the use of materials. In many periods it was also the mark of an educated person to know something about architecture and to show an appreciation of fine things.

The more immediate roots of design education in schools can be found in the nineteenth century. Professional design training in engineering and architecture was obtained by attachment to a design office and the art schools had been founded to train applied artists but there was Government concern about the skills of the working classes. Apprenticeships and learning on the job were fine up to a point, but many left school without any skills relevant to employment. And what about girls? Were they competent to be the wives and mothers of the labour force needed by industry and the Empire? People in power were doubtful and the result was the emergence of Woodwork and Metalwork and the beginnings of Domestic Science, later Home Economics. These continued in very traditional form until at least the 1960s when, in company with Art and Design there was a move to bring them into the modern world of mass production, the media and consumerism. These were the subjects which, from the late Sixties onwards were the main protagonists in the development of design education. Never a particularly compatible grouping, subject rivalries were set to do much harm to the infant design education 'movement'. In the then new National Curriculum design found itself divided between two subject areas: Art and Design and Design and Technology. The Design and Technology Working Group struggled to incorporate forward thinking but were partly defeated by the Government's crass model of Attainment Targets and Programmes of Study. Imagination and creativity, essential to design, proved very hard to pin down.

Home Economics suffered particularly badly. Successive Governments whittled away at child care, textiles and cooking until food became just another 'material' in Design and Technology. The irony is that this was happening just when there was growing concern over standards of parenting and unhealthy eating habits. School meals declined in standard along with the teaching of cooking. Cooking is back and this is to be welcomed but the real prize would be for it to be the central focus of a new Food curriculum. Potentially, this could become part of a larger curriculum segment to do with human development. Anita Cormac explores the nature of Food education below.

A FRESH START FOR FOOD EDUCATION

Anita Cormac
Food education consultant
Founder and Director of the Focus on Food Campaign

Food education is poised to take a new position. Its importance is now recognized by Government and has the backing of health and social science professionals. The national problem – an obeseogenic population – gives urgency to the establishment of an up-to-date food curriculum for all age groups and supported by well-trained teachers. Before that can become a reality, however, there needs to be a complete re-think of teaching and learning about food. The key will be to build the pupil's experience around practical cooking activities but with perspectives looking outwards to diet and health; agriculture and sustainability; and the role of the active consumer.

Food education potentially offers a unique blend of innovation and conservation, respecting past culinary traditions and adapting them to the diverse needs of contemporary society. Food is a matter of survival. Food involves every individual making decisions and choices every day. Teaching about food needs to begin at an early age when tastes and personal preferences are beginning to emerge. At the centre of learning is the 'creative capability' that is the hallmark of cooking skill and beyond that food knowledge, food culture and nutrition.

Although domestic cooking involves 'designerly thinking' and commercial food companies certainly design new food products, food and cooking do not seem to have benefited from their association with the design curriculum. In education, cooking is best seen as an essential life skill. Subject credibility is not dependent on association with science, economics or design. Food education has intrinsic value and should have its own place in the general education curriculum.

Before detailed content can be established, there will need to be a new consensus on the rationale and specific value framework that underlies food. This will need to be related to the potential of each age group. Teacher training and professional development will be needed to support any new curriculum. Primary teachers are not food specialists and are acutely in need of support and training. Secondary food technology teachers now need a period of updating, reflection and flexibility in order to take an active and leading role in future developments. The potential verve and vitality of a new food curriculum demands high calibre, dynamic training aimed at culinary competence.

Design education in schools has enjoyed the support of design professionals. This is important for the future but general education needs to be cautious about any attempt by engineers, architects or the creative industries to dictate a top down curriculum model as has happened in the past. Generally this has been because of a lack of communication between educationalists and professional designers. It is important for the various professionals not to try to outbid each other in their attempts to achieve a curriculum 'relevant' to their industry. A point that needs making frequently is that it is only a part of the job of design educators to prepare future professionals, equally important is fostering a design aware public equipped with designerly skills relevant to their own lives and the needs of the community.

Closer links between schools and design professionals, including those involved in advertising, retailing and marketing, would help inter-professional cooperation and bring a useful breath of the world of work and business into schools. Any such collaboration needs clear aims. Fortunately there exist several models of good practice. Eileen Adams describes her work with architects and planners on p27.

At the highest level, designerly talent is as unusual as musical or literary genius. But as with music and language, design ability is also a universal attribute of human beings. People have always used their designerly skills in creating a domestic environment and often in their everyday work. In the past such skills were usually developed 'on the job', cooking was learnt in the kitchen, work skill in an apprenticeship, formal or informal.

Studies of children's mental abilities, and particularly their rich imaginative lives, show that they develop designerly abilities at a very early stage. Neuroscience suggests that the basic ability to design and understand design is hard-wired in humans but that it expresses itself in a great diversity of ways depending on experience, education and culture.

The ability to imagine and model alternative futures has been made potent by the exponential growth of science and technology. Design ability pushes technology forward but also domesticates it. Design, since the industrial revolution, has played a key role in bringing technology to market. In a free market economy, design has found a dynamic and volatile partner. Together they have transformed everyday life, created wealth and helped to turn society upside-down.

The human ability to imagine alternative futures has been made all the more important because science and technology now provide society with tools to bring irreversible change. The speed with which the forms of things unknown become known and tangible was accelerated to a point where cultural, social and moral frameworks find it hard to keep up.

INTERPROFESSIONAL IN COLLABORATION IN DESIGN EDUCATION

Eileen Adams

The environment is part of our everyday experience: architecture, design and planning are not subjects that only experts know about. However, most teachers are not trained in these disciplines, and feel at a disadvantage when they are expected to teach about them. Environmental design projects are as much about *how* you learn as *what* you learn. The challenge is to engage with questions of how we choose to live and how we decide to shape our environment.

Models for learning in environmental design are those that involve experiential, investigative and project-based learning, where students are required to gather, sort, and classify information, suggest hypotheses and test them. An important element is critical study, to explain and justify choices, judgements and decisions. Synthesis is achieved through design activity. Teachers bring into play their knowledge of how young people learn and strategies for supporting learning. Inspirational leadership is at the basis of all good learning and teaching, and the teacher who is a keen enthusiast will inspire pupils to explore and experiment. Most importantly, the teacher's role is modelling how to learn, and how to make use of the results of that learning.

Collaboration with architects, planners and landscape architects can extend and enrich what schools can do for themselves. Designers are able to:

- Make a significant contribution to conceptualising and planning projects, suggesting possibilities for study and ways of handling topics.
- Provide resources such as maps and plans.
- Introduce topics for study, identifying unfamiliar concepts and vocabulary and exploring unfamiliar ideas.
- Support streetwork sessions, explaining how to use the study methods, analyse and appraise townscape quality and record information.
- Support design activity, guiding pupils through different stages of appraisal, ideas generation, development of ideas and presentation of proposals.
- Share techniques used in professional design practice and demonstrate ways of handling computer-aided design.
- Engage in critique of students' work, both during the design activities and at the final presentations.

Students are the third partner in the collaboration. They bring a sense of excitement and discovery, as well as local knowledge of their environment. They enjoy learning from first-hand experience and take pleasure in study that is purposeful, where they have ownership of the ideas. They value opportunities to contribute to thinking about the changing environment, to share the results of their efforts and are proud their voices can be heard.

Nearly forty years ago, Bruce Archer told a government sponsored conference about education that it was his 'sincere conviction' that a 'massive broadening and deepening of design education in secondary schools … is overwhelmingly the most urgent need for the survival as well as the happiness of mankind'. It was an extraordinarily bold claim. The time has come to put forward that claim once again. But I would make an addition. In my view the pre-requisite for a 'massive broadening and deepening of design education in secondary schools' is to do the same for primary schools.

In case the concerns of 1973 seem remote and irrelevant, Bruce made his claim for design education against a background of economic difficulties, environmental crises and social uncertainty. He spoke of 'the four great crises facing mankind'. The first three are immediately recognizable:

- the crisis of overpopulation;
- the crisis of pollution;
- the crisis of depletion of natural resources.

None of these has gone away. To them Bruce added a fourth:

- the crisis of control.

This does not resonate so immediately but it turns out to be very topical indeed. Bruce was highlighting the disillusion and alienation that many people experience in contemporary society. He spoke of unintended consequences and catastrophic accidents resulting from rapid technological innovation; of institutions, such as banks, out of control; of environmental and social decay.

Bruce lamented the loss of 'traditional values'. I have never been a great enthusiast for these, nor do I subscribe to a romantic vision of the past. In many aspects of life, the present is measurably more liberal and successful than most of the past. However, what still rings true today is people's anxiety about the future and their lack of confidence in our collective ability to act for the collective good. We are anxious because we seem not to have a coherent vision of a desirable future and, worse still, doubt our ability to bring it about.

In 1973, governments had begun to take design seriously but it was on the economic significance of design that they focused. Educationalists followed their lead. Of course Bruce recognised the economic significance of design but it is clear that he also had something of wide significance in mind. I believe he chose his words with care: he was talking about a wider set of environmental, social and psychological values. I am impressed by the fact that he refers not only to the survival of mankind but to its happiness. What did he mean? Surely he was thinking of design ability and design awareness as antidotes to the alienation and sense of powerlessness inherent in the 'crisis of control'. In 'designerly thinking' he saw one of the few cognitive media capable of coming to grips with an uncertain future.

My own recent work strongly bears out this view. Over the past ten years, I have tried to understand what happens in the mind when somebody is designing. I have tried to look at designing from four different perspectives:

- evolutionary biology;
- neuroscience;
- cultural history;
- child development.

Evolutionary biology and neuroscience have provided the most general framework. The way we use our 'big brain' comes from our evolutionary history which, in turn, has 'hard-wired' capacities and potentials which express themselves in distinctive ways in different cultures. Children follow a pattern of growth which is partly hard-wired but which is also influenced by the culture into which they are born.

'Designerly thinking' turns out to be a key element in the story of humanity. Evolutionary biologists characterize us as occupying a 'cognitive niche' in evolution. We are able to construct 'causal models' of the world and to use these models flexibly and creatively in our mind's eye in our responses to the environment. Seen in this context 'designerly thinking' is a further niche within the wider cognitive niche. It is precisely this kind of thinking that has enabled us to construct the made environment within the natural environment.

Designerly thinking expresses itself in a variety of ways. If I list a few of them, please use your own ability at mental modelling to see them in your own mind's eye:

- I can sketch the future, perhaps on a napkin at a dinner
- I can talk about it, perhaps with like-minded colleagues, but also in a formal presentation trying to persuade a client
- I can make rough models of my idea, making it visible to myself
- I can make an exquisitely detailed model of it, so realistic that we can imagine using it or walking through it
- I can express its proposed structure in mathematical models
- I can represent its proposed performance in charts and diagrams
- I can 'run it' in a computer simulation
- I can write a detailed specification supported by comprehensive working drawings so that you can go ahead and manufacture it
- I can create an illustrated story about the kind of person that might want to use and buy my proposed product
- I can make a story board for a film showing how sound, vision, set and story can be brought together
- I can model the hoped-for economic performance of a design proposal
- I can build a prototype and try it out
- I can invite users to do their thing with prototypes or mock-ups
- I can even engage in large-scale experiments with real people and real places or products.

I argue that in the light of the problems facing humanity, our current approach to the curriculum is fatally flawed. As a nation, we continue to emphasise the acquisition of knowledge rather than the exercise of the imagination. We continue to emphasise the acquisition of knowledge rather than the creative application of knowledge. We continue to emphasise knowledge of the past at the expense of learning how to shape – and control – the future.

The traditions of Design and Technology and Art and Design mean that they are well placed to take a lead in developing the kind of curriculum we need. There are also other perspectives. There are design education opportunities in Geography and Science and importantly with the development of the 'skilled consumer' in Citizenship and Home Economics. Design can be viewed in the context of history and design activity contributes decisively to cultural history.

In order to occupy the vacant space in the curriculum, design education needs to be clear about its own values and distinctive styles of teaching, learning and assessment. It also needs to begin to map out progression and development from nursery to sixth form. In inviting leading academics to write on the seven themes that I identified in my John Eggleston lecture, the aim is to make a substantial contribution to the intellectual foundations of design education. We hope these are a firm basis for a future curriculum.

The seven themes are:

1   The aims of design education
2   The significance of practical education
3   Encouraging the imagination
4   The cognitive value of aesthetic awareness
5   The value of learning through making
6   The creative relationships between designing and making
7   The educational purpose of doing design projects

1. THE AIMS OF DESIGN EDUCATION ... *Ken Baynes*

Design education has always found itself squeezed by subject rivalries and by two apparently conflicting goals. Should priority be given to nurturing future design professionals or to providing the mass of people with access to designerly skills and knowledge about design? The response to this dilemma has generally been to go for a watered down version of professional design education. This top-down approach has led to some excellent practice and particularly at the upper end of secondary schools allows gifted students the opportunity to do outstanding work.

I have been equally excited by some of the pioneering work in Primary schools. Triggered by the National Curriculum, it showed that children could engage in designerly thinking at their own level of skill, knowledge and experience. Teachers worked on a 'bottom up' approach that built on insights into children's minds and particularly their emerging imaginative capacity. So far this kind of practice is the exception rather than the rule but it provides an encouraging glimpse of the potential in young children.

A future curriculum could emerge from these two areas of excellent practice. Part of the development work needed would be to create a bridge between the two.

Aims need to be relatively simple and something like the following might be an effective framework:
- To provide pupils and teachers with a challenging, absorbing, entertaining and satisfying opportunity to work and study together
- To give every child the opportunity to learn about design and designing at their own level
- To give pupils with particular aptitude in design the opportunity to develop their ability as the basis for a possible career in an area related to art, design, engineering, craft or technology
- To provide every child with design skills and knowledge relevant to adult life, particularly home-making, the environment, self -expression and social engagement.

At the same time I would want to shift the centre of gravity in the curriculum towards the environment. I would highlight not only our responsibility towards the natural environment but equally the extraordinary significance of the made environment. We shape it and it shapes us.

The approach to design education for everyone could begin by rethinking the idea of 'consumer education'. Consumers are now seen as passive choosers, shuffling the pack of goodies on offer in stores, garages and estate agents. See them instead as proactive. It would be good to re-christen them 'domestic designers', shaping their own lives and their own environment. Beyond personal and family health and well-being should come a positive attitude to the future with a growing sense of the effectiveness of thinking globally and acting locally. The ability to visualise, discuss and work towards the future depends on learning modelling skills and developing the imagination.

THE AIMS OF DESIGN EDUCATION

Phil Roberts

First, some scene-setting:

1 In the 1970s, Professor Bruce Archer revisited the idea that there is a third area in education (equivalent in significance to Science and the Humanities) concerned with the making and doing aspects of human activity. He called it Design. It was not a new idea: Archer noted its distinguished tradition through William Morris, Saint Thomas Aquinas and going back to Plato[1].   (We could, though, note in passing that 'doing and making' was not (and is not) an entirely sufficient shorthand phrase, and certainly design educationists could argue that 'doing, making, and being' might well be a better one.)

But never mind any possible insufficiences – the notion of a third area in education remains fundamental and significant - Archer argued that:

'Design, in its most general educational sense, where it is equated with Science and the Humanities, is defined as the area of human experience, skill and understanding that reflects man's concern with the appreciation and adaption of his surroundings in the light of his material and spiritual needs. In particular, though not exclusively, it relates with configuration, composition, meaning, value and purpose in man-made phenomena. We can then go on to adopt, as an equivalent to literacy and numeracy, the term 'design awareness', which thus means 'the ability to understand and handle those ideas which are expressed through the medium of doing and making'. The question of the language in which such ideas may be expressed is an interesting one. The essential language of Science is notation, especially mathematical notation. The essential language of the Humanities is natural language, especially written language. The essential language of Design is modelling. A model is a representation of something. An artist's painting is a representation of an idea he is trying to explore. A gesture in mime is a representation of some idea. Everyone engaged in the handling of ideas in the fine arts, performing arts, useful arts or technology employs models or representations to capture, analyse, explore and transmit those ideas. Just as the vocabulary and syntax of natural language or of scientific notation can be conveyed through spoken sounds, words on paper, semaphore signals, Morse code or electronic digits, to suit convenience, so that the vocabulary and syntax of the modelling of ideas in the Design area can be conveyed through a variety of media such as drawings, diagrams, physical representations, gestures, algorithms - not to mention natural language and scientific notation ...' (nd, early 1970s, p 6)

---

1 Archer pursued notions fundamental to developing design education through a series of conference papers in the 1970s arising, primarily, from the work conducted in the Department of Design Research at the Royal College of Art for the DES-sponsored research inquiry 'Design in General Education'. Professor Archer was at that time Head of the Department of Design Research; subsequently he was the RCA's Director of Research.

Archer continued:

'The repository of knowledge in Science is not only the literature of science but also the analytical skills and the intellectual integrity of which the scientist is the guardian. The repository of knowledge in the Humanities is not simply the literature of the humanities but also the discursive skills and the spiritual values of which the scholar is the guardian. In Design, the repository of knowledge is not only the material culture and the contents of the museums but also the executive skills of the doer and maker.' (op cit, p6)

Without going into the subsequent and necessarily larger conversation that accompanied this fresh look at a third area of education, it is enough (at any rate, for our purposes here) to note that the coverage of the concept, Design, refers to the existence of a vast and diverse field of human activity, behaviour, and enterprise. In its specialist manifestations, for instance, we readily recognise that Design ranges between the craft-based artefact to product and engineering design based in digital high-technologies; from fashion design to various areas of communication design; from component to product to systems design; from buildings and architecture to place and environment; that it makes use of two- and three-dimensional forms and media; using traditional materials, new man-made materials, and new technologies; and, indeed, in principle, that it makes use of whatever kinds of knowledge and whatever kinds of technology are necessary to the pursuit of the designer's objectives.

Specialist practitioners also use particular *specialist languages of discourse*. We should note that especially because, when it comes to the consideration of general education, there is a need to be wary of believing that specialist disciplines and areas of professional practice should, or can, inevitably inform the nature, the principles and practices of design-educational activity in *general education*. It is not part of the general case for providing design education as a part of general education, that acting out the role of designer is necessarily a good or appropriate thing for school children to do. Nor is it a strong part of the general case simply to assert, say, that the production of an artefact is the necessary outcome of educational activity. Rather, the achieving of any such product relates to their roles as *a means* towards *an educational end*: hence, we appraise the achievement in the pupil rather than appraise only the product.

2 Let's run with *Design* as indicative of the overarching and encompassing parental ground.

Then, the term *design education* refers, overall, to that set of (school) subject areas, to Further Education (FE) and Higher Education (HE) curricular & course provision, and to professional-specialist areas and disciplines of designing, which have the object of educating and training pupils, students, would-be professional practitioners, and citizens in general with regard to the world of Design. Or as Archer put it in a paper presented to Midland Art Advisors:

'The fostering of sensibility, understanding and skill in the area of design is a proper and fundamental function of general education. Like the other strands

35

of education, those of design sensibility, design understanding and design skill are woven into the texture of the school organisation and curriculum, and may or may not be isolated as faculties, departments and/or subjects in their own rights.' (1975, p1)

In this paper, *design education* is deliberately further delimited: it is used with reference only to the design-related education of pupils in full-time *general* education between the ages of 5 and 16. This delimiting is essential for the reader to observe. GCSE subject courses, A-level curricula and courses, Further Education, together with Higher Education curricula and courses exhibit a progressively greater degrees of specialist and disciplinary/area focus, specificity, intention, and required outcomes. That is, the participants (children/young students); the nature, the intentions/objects (viz, of personal and cognitive development); and the subject courses of 5-16 general education must be carefully distinguished from those of more-specialist and subsequent educational programmes. An unwitting conflation, based on too-easily accepted assumptions about similarity between apparently similar activities (but not so similar intentions) and on notions of 'progression' can lead to a confusion that is helpful neither to general education nor to later provision.

3 The title of this paper, 'The Aims of Design Education', also carries a potential pitfall for the unwary insofar as its shorthand might suggest that an abstraction ('Design Education') has (or, indeed, can have) Aims. More properly (or pedantically), it is *people* who pursue aims & objectives. Hence, the title is to be understood, rather, as *'The objects of engaging in designer-like activity in general education'*. This, too, begs a few questions; we'll try to resolve them as we go along.

4   Some axiomatic preliminaries that arise (and which, given the space, could be substantiated):

- *that the capacities for the comprehension, and engagement with, the phenomena of design, and for engaging in purposeful acting in and on the world – ie, designing - are universal human capacities.* That is, they are not the possessions of only a gifted few individuals, nor are they 'owned' by members of specialist design professional communities. (It follows that any needs peculiar to the 'gifted few', or of the eventual specialist practitioner, should be subsumed within a general education that meets the needs of all pupils, rather than that design in general education be led by or predicated primarily on the needs and practices of small minorities. And it follows further, that the specialist education & training of specialist professional designers should not be thought inevitably or necessarily to provide the best model for design education in 5-16 general education.)

- *that,* on this view, *designing – or, engaging in intentional human activity – is central to being-in-the-world, to the development of mind and cognition, to human being, to the making of meaning and values, and indeed to the pursuit of all human enterprise.* (That is or course the case whether or not such activity is recognised and addressed in educational curricula or in school subject courses.) Put simply, immersion in designing-learning changes the agent of the activity (the pupil) and some aspect of the world. That is, *change* of some kind (in capabiity, sensibility, knowledge, whatever) is a key (required) outcome of design-educational activity; but further, *the world is also changed* as a consequence of design activity (or intentional activity).

- *that cognitive modelling is the essential medium, or 'language', of designing (or, of acting on and in the world). That is, such modelling* (or presentation and representation of ideas, of aspirations, of visions of future but presently unknown possibilities in various forms and media, etc) *is central to and a distinctive characteristic of designing and, therefore, the development of modelling capabilities and models is necessarily at the core of design education (see Roberts (1992) for some discussion of cognitive modelling).*

- *that the structure and structuring of designing and of learning - ie, designing-learning - are based on similar logics* but, nevertheless, some seeming similarities should not lead to the illogical assumption that there are straight-forwardly interchangeable intentions or elements of content between professional design practices and the practices of general education.

- *that 'doing and making (and being)' - or, action-based learning & teaching - provide the crucial enabling and required experience and conditions for developing design capability, design cognition & intelligence, design sensibility & awareness, etc.* That is, purposefully engaging in 'design problems' (or, alternatively put, addressing experienced (and problematic) states-of-affairs that require some change) brings about, first, developmental changes in the pupil and, second, some change in the pupils' world. (The first is essential in a would-be educative environment; the second may or may not also be a required outcome. On this view, pupils' experience in general education may indeed have some apparent resonance with the intentions and the outcomes of the specialist design practitioner's work.)

- *that the core content, or the principal objects of attention, of a design educational curriculum, or courses, should be 'problematised' for the purposes of participant teaching & learning.* That is, core learning-&-teaching experience would consist in pupils articulating and addressing problematic *states-of-affairs* (including needs, wants, and aspirations) from within their own experience and circumstances that, being resolved sufficiently (ie, against agreed criteria), would develop their analytical abilities and operational competencies, the making of meanings, and judging between competing values; or, more generally expressed, would bring about change in themselves and in their worlds. These are commonly referred to as 'design problems', or as problem solving. That said, there is of course a proper place for pupils to engage also with *puzzles* (which, by definition, have assured solutions, provided the rules are followed), along with *tasks* and *exercises*: it is the complexities of *design problems* (or ill-defined states-of-affairs, however, that ultimately provide the substantive foci of teaching and learning attention).

And, two more axiomatic propositions - on another level and from a quite different point of view:

- *that the design education curriculum – at a high level of generality as well as at the low levels of specificity in particular courses – along with design pedagogy, design-related school curricular subjects, and, essentially, the institutional circumstances & conditions of schools should be developed*; (noting, in passing, that that final feature is rarely considered with any realism in any educational policy innovation).

- *that*, more particularly and derived from the above, *design education should be the object of continuous review & development on the part, primarily, of participant design-based teachers. That is, curricular review & development should be institutionalised and, indeed, exemplified in pedagogic approaches and course content.* That, of course, is a radical notion; it sounds a very tall order indeed, though is manifestly not impossible, and in the long term would have considerable benefits.

5 So now to the point - 'the objects of engaging in designer-like activity in 5-16 general education'. Alternatively, we might prefer to respond to questions such as: '*Why* provide design education for the 5-16 age range?' or, '*How*, at a high-level of generality, can the heart of such a design education be characterised?'

The essential object, perhaps, is simply to provide the opportunities and conditions in schools so that pupils and teachers:

- *will be participant in teaching & learning such that developmental changes will be effected in pupils' overall personal and cognitive development and,* more specifically, *in their design capabilities, in their design knowledge understanding; and in their appreciation of the fundamental roles and functions of cognitive modelling* (as revealed through the use of a variety of forms, technology, and media).

- *will be participant in teaching & learning such that pupils will experience, and appreciate, that their learning-through-designing* (and others', together with the work of professional design disciplines) *brings about changes not only in themselves but also in the societal-cultural environment, and in the external material world, (and, indeed, that such activity creates and changes the immediate material culture and has qualitative impacts and far-reaching effects on the wider cultural and physical environments).*

and, more particularly:

- *will be enabled through guided and heuristic engagement in participant teaching and learning) to identify, articulate, and resolve problematic states-of-affairs (ie, design problems) derived from, and significant to, their own lives.* This is the core of any design-based curriculum and course, irrespective of the courses' subject area within the field of Design.

[It's worth expanding on the nature and asserted centrality of problem-solving in design education and in its curricular courses so as to get some sense of why such activity is seen as having such potential in design education and teaching & learning:

'Problem solving and ill-defined problems are to do with engaging-in the real world. In the world of education and in the practices of design pedagogy such problems may be variously charaterised (if not defined) as:

existential: that is, they are to with individual and social creation of meanings, identity and values; having open or fuzzy 'boundaries'; being located in a societal-cultural matrix view of human action (subsuming the activity specified as design activity); requiring heuristic activity to resolve.

Additionally, it can be suggested that ill-defined problems have properties such as:

an uncertainty in the propriety of the grounds upon which decision-making might be made: that is, the grounds are unclear and cannot be generalized from no matter how many particular instances there are;

a uniqueness: that is, the problems are situation-contingent, and unique in particulars that cannot be exhaustively and generally nominated and specified;

an involvement with compromise: that is, their articulation and their resolution require judging between possibly (and probably) competing criteria; or, put differently, valueing is central; and

an unpredictability of outcome: that is, we cannot predict, precisely, the outcome of our taking action.'   (Roberts, 1992, p207)]

This is descriptive of the basic human learning activity. To return to our theme from this digression, and to continue, the objects of design education are to provide the conditions and experience such that teachers and pupils:

- *will be enabled to engage in valueing, and to identify values and design-based qualities – including personal, group, cultural, environmental, economic, and societal – that emerge as integral and necessary considerations in designing-learning (or, even, that emerge as drivers of designing), and which are core* to design/learning activity together with their contribution to the making of personal identity, meaning, and values.

- *will be enabled to appreciate the roles and the functions of designing (and the impact and effects of design outcomes, (some of them, incidentally, being unintended) in, explicitly, different contexts (eg, the economic, the cultural-societal, the family, the school, etc); and will appreciate the outcomes of design activity from the perspectives of 'the designer', 'the maker', 'the user', 'the observer', and 'the man-(or-woman)-in-the-street'.* This is also to say that pupils' consideration of *the various contexts of design activity* are crucial aspects of effective and satisfying design competence and sensibility. (Within this - and it is a very particular instance of design attention - when considering *function, use, and value,* pupils would learn to distinguish between *utilitarian function* and *esteem function*, this being non-trivial in the appraisal and purchase of, for instance, many consumer and fashion articles; and, also, the concept and reality of *cost v value-for-money* (or 'What are we prepared to pay for X or Y?'))

6 Finally, if we accept the broad meanings of Design, and designing, and design education; the structural and logical similarities between (i) learning and (ii) designing in general education; and would wish to elevate Design to the status of the third main axis of general education, there arise practical matters of implementation. Briefly – because it is not the subject of this paper – there is already in place a mixed economy of practice and possibility on which to build. That is, we could pursue design as a school subject in its own right (as happens, to some extent, beyond the 5-16 general education curriculum), pursuing its own truths and developing its own tradition and methods; or pursue design phenomena as subject matter, or objects of attention, that incidentally intersect with any other school subject. Whichever, the need for educational development is obvious.

2. THE SIGNIFICANCE OF PRACTICAL EDUCATION ... *Ken Baynes*

Biologists characterise *homo sapiens sapiens* as occupying the 'cognitive niche' in evolution. This might suggest that, in human intelligence, theory comes first and is superior to practice. In fact, this is not the case. The essence of human intelligence is not only to link theory and practice but also to learn from experience. Gaining experience is crucially a matter of acting in and on the world. Human beings have developed the art of advancing theory by means of practice and experiment.

Humans 'try things out'. They do this not only in the arts, science and design and technology but also in every other sphere of life from social organisation and politics to sexual behaviour and personal relationships. In many fields of human endeavour 'trying it out' - practice - is the key to the advancement of knowledge and a driving force for 'progress'.

Evolutionary theory, neuroscience and studies of child development all go to show that it is a fundamental error to separate theory from practice in education. In most human activities, theory develops partly from practice and practice changes in response to theory. In many areas of learning, practice cannot in fact be learnt from a study of theory. It is, for example, impossible to learn how to drive a car until you actually sit in a driving seat. Books on how to drive – or the teacher's verbal instructions – only make sense when they can be tried out in the real situation. On the other hand, if we want to learn about the history of motoring or the physical and engineering principles behind the internal combustion engine, it is necessary to turn to the store of knowledge on the subject.

In the case of design, I would argue that the only way to learn how to design is by actually designing. On the other hand, if you want to learn about the history of design, then books, museums, documents, TV programmes and designed things (amongst other sources) will be essential providers of information. Knowing about the history of design may also make you a more creative and fluent designer.

This difference used to be called the difference between knowing HOW and knowing THAT. The two are clearly interdependent but it turns out that there is a further dimension to the psychology of learning beyond either proficiency in a skill or the accumulation of knowledge. It is knowing WHY. The most powerful educational experience is to have the excitement and satisfaction of applying both skill and knowledge to achieve a worthwhile goal. It is in the PURPOSEFUL application of both skill and knowledge that the true relevance of education is made clear.

We now often talk of a knowledge-based society. Governments all over the world have realized that somehow the economic wealth of society is related to the amount of knowledge in it. But this subtly misses the point. The crux for a successful economy is not knowledge itself (though knowledge must be there) but the ability to deploy knowledge creatively in responding to and shaping change. Unlike the majority of the school curriculum, which emphasises what is already known, there also needs to be an emphasis on making the future. Three key questions worth asking pupils are: 'How did it come to be like that?'; 'What value has it now?'; and 'How should it be in the future?'. The first emphasises the known, the second calls for critical analysis and judgement while the third encourages speculation and imagination and the application of knowledge and practical skills to human needs.

THE SIGNIFICANCE OF PRACTICAL EDUCATION

Eddie Norman, then Ken Baynes

'What is the significance of different ways of knowing?

One way of giving direction to the discussion of this theme emerges from this reformulation. It makes apparent the central nature of epistemological issues in this context. Having made some headway on what the underlying categories might be, it becomes possible to reflect on their significance, but this is awkward territory as indicated by Janet Daley in her 1984 paper entitled *Design creativity and the understanding of objects*. Towards the end of this paper she writes;

> 'Perhaps my most controversial claim would be that all of the propositional knowledge (and consequent reasoning) which we take to be the content of our intellectual activity is but the small intersection of a set of systems. That is, the mind may not have a systematic way of knowing or conceiving, the schemata of which can be definitively described, but it may have a number of innate capacities for constructing schemata, the logics of which may only minimally overlap, i.e. be translatable into the terms of others. Thus, conscious mental activity, with its language-based emphasis on propositional knowledge may be the area in which these various systems intersect with that of verbal discourse.'
> (p299)

In the conclusions to her paper the implications of this claim are developed:

> 'To talk of propositional knowledge in this area, or to make knowledge claims about the thinking processes of designers, may be fundamentally wrong-headed. The way designers work may be inexplicable, not for some romantic or mystical reason, but simply because these processes lie outside the bounds of verbal discourse: they are literally indescribable in linguistic terms.' (p300)

So this paper is essentially about alluding to matters that could be 'indescribable in linguistic terms' and it is perhaps therefore unsurprising that the significance of practical education has been at the centre of continual controversy not only in design education, but in general education debates. To get on to some solid ground, the discussion starts in one particular design area ... acoustic guitar design.

ACOUSTIC GUITAR DESIGN

It is possible to know about acoustic guitars in many ways. It is possible to know that the guitar evolved from the lute families of instruments in Spain in the 13th century, and that 309 woods – from Abura to Zebrawood - have been found to be useful, as well as their properties and applications (Jahnel, 1981). It is possible to know that there are five key elements that define the technical performance of the acoustic guitar: the strings; the neck and fingerboard; the top; the bridge; and the size, shape and kinds of materials of the body (Huber, 1994, p 31). It is possible to know that acoustic guitars fall into one of 'four families of design: classical, flamenco, flat top (or folk) and arch top' (Fletcher & Rossing, 1998, p239) and that they can:

' … be considered to be a system of coupled vibrators … At low frequency, the top plate transmits energy to the back via both the ribs and the air cavity; the bridge essentially acts as part of the top plate. At high frequency, however, most of the sound is radiated by the top plate, and the mechanical properties of the bridge may become significant.' (ibid, p240)

It is possible know that the top plate has particular modes of vibration at different frequencies, to measure the frequencies and photograph the modes of vibration in holographic interferograms. And much more besides, as documented by, for example, the *Catgut Acoustic Society*, *American Lutherie* and the *Journal of Guitar Acoustics*. However, in the context of acoustic guitar design where does this lead to? Bernard Richardson, of Cardiff University, is a foremost authority on guitar physics and a guitar maker. This quotation indicates the limitations associated with this kind of knowledge.

'Because no two pieces of wood are alike, even … from the same tree, the maker has to fashion each piece of wood in an individual way to exploit its maximum advantage … there is no substitute for the sensibilities of the skilled craftsman who has learned through long experience how to extract the required vibrations from carefully chosen and carefully fashioned pieces of wood. It is these makers who are the key to the future prosperity of the instrument.'
(1994, p10)

'Knowing that …', in the context of acoustic guitar design, is fascinating , as evidenced by the immense efforts that have been made by humans to attain knowledge of the history of the guitar, its evolution, construction and physics. And it is useful knowledge, but not sufficient for creative activity. For analysts, such as museum curators and connoisseurs, and for guitarists there is no need to go further, but for guitar making there must also be 'know how'. A formal training as a luthier – guitar maker – would usually involve the replication of a 'Torres construction guitar'. Understanding why this is so takes us closer to understanding the elusive concept of 'knowing how'. Torres was a guitar maker in Spain in the nineteenth century and his work had a dramatic influence on the evolution of the guitar as this quotation indicates.

'The instruments played by Sor and his famous contemporaries – Dionisio Aguado (1784-1849) and Matteo Carcassi (1792-1853), for instance – were, however, far inferior to the guitars at the disposal of today's players. All that changed – with a quantum jump in the development of classical guitar construction – at the hands of a carpenter from San Sebastian de Almeria, Antonio de Torres Jurado (1817-1892). Better known simply as Torres, he was without a doubt the most important figure in the history of guitar design and construction. Musicians who played his guitars immediately discarded those of other makers. Throughout Spain luthiers adopted Torres' designs. In fact, to this day, classical guitar makers still construct their instruments in the manner of Torres.' (Denyer, 1982:42)

Torres increased the scale length of the guitar to 650mm and developed guitar bodies which were larger and deeper, but not heavier, introduced improved fan strutting and a slightly domed, or arched, top. These crucial changes resulted in 'high volume and good quality tonal response in all registers' (Chapman, 1993:22). As noted by Jahnel, Torres used the musical intervals of Pythagoras to determine some of the dimensions.

> 'An excellent example of this design method is given by the famous La Leona (1858) guitar. Upper bout to waist are in the ratio 9:8 (Second); upper bout to lower bout is 3:4 (Fourth); waist to lower bout is 2:3 (Fifth). A large number of his guitars only show Pythagoras' intervals in unimportant measurements …)'
> (1981:109)

The use of such ratios has no particular scientific foundation and is an illustration of the 'mystery' that still surrounds the design and construction of musical instruments. In order to understand this mystery – or the 'know how' embodied in a Torres construction guitar a little more deeply, consider Huber's discussion of the issues below.

> 'The Torres system has obviously achieved such success because it works. It offers a way around a fundamental difficulty in guitar making. If a piece of wood, a brace or a top for example, is to be thinned, only experience can really indicate where this should be done. Thinning a piece of wood makes it lighter. This could raise its resonant frequency by lowering its mass. Thinning the piece could also reduce its stiffness, thereby lowering the frequency of resonance. Removing wood in hope of raising a resonance could therefore both lower resonance and weaken the structure if the maker is unfortunate in his choice of where to cut. The theoretical knowledge to understand and deal with this problem is not yet formulated and part of the guitar making tradition, but a body of practical knowledge based on a century of experience with Torres type fan bracing does exist and is available. It is also especially well suited to permitting or even encouraging small modifications within the basic structural concept, so users of the Torres system can both benefit from the experience of traditional guitar making, and create sufficient variation to adjust it to their own style of construction. Except for experimental purposes, there is no apparent or obvious need for the guitar maker to look elsewhere for a bracing system, especially if he is a professional who must guard his reputation and earn his living by selling his own production.'   (1994, pp 40-41)

Torres built many prototypes in order to achieve an understanding of the construction methods he developed, including one with the back and sides made from papier-mâché in order to demonstrate that it was the front that was the most significant contributor to the guitar's sound. He achieved remarkable success, and, consequently, from a technical perspective, there is a strong tendency to stay close to his designs. From a cultural point of view, there are equally strong reasons not to stray too far. The guitar's rise to popularity in the sixteenth century is often associated with the poet Vincente Espinel.

'Soon (the Spanish guitar) seemed to be everywhere, rapidly overshadowing the fragile and more complicated lute. Alarmed purists and lute lovers condemned the guitar, trying to give it a bad name by associating it with undignified frolicking in the streets, unrestrained body movements and a general spirit of joyful, sensual abandon. The more the guitar was identified with such pursuits, the more it dominated folk music in Europe. Romantics loved to serenade with it, ladies loved to hear it, painters loved to paint it. Those were grim days for lute makers.'   (Wheeler, 1981)

The semantic associations of the guitar form with romance and rebellion have their origins long before the 1960s when it became synonymous with the anti-war protest movements and the folk revival. Some of the guitars of that period were 'nylon strung' and it would be possible to trace their roots directly back to Torres, but others were 'metal strung' with stronger bracing patterns under the soundboard to withstand the increased string tension. These were derived from the work of American makers, such as Christian Friedrich Martin (1796-1873). He brought his knowledge of European practice to America when he arrived in 1831, having been a foreman in Johann Staufer's shop in Vienna. The early guitars he made in America maintained their European influences, but over a period of 15-20 years his own designs emerged, most notably the cross- or X-braced top, which has become as important in the 'know how' of steel strung guitars as Torres' construction is for nylon strung guitars. Nevertheless, when looked at 'from the outside' the form echoes down the centuries. So, the 'know how' to be successful in a cultural sense is also well established.

Modern luthiers know how to make high quality instruments; they know that their instruments fall into particular historical and musical categories, and they know that they function in particular ways. They also know why they are constructed as they are, both in a technical and cultural sense. Some can, if they choose to, rise above the apparent constraints and move beyond creating traditional instruments to innovate. One such luthier is Rob Armstrong of Coventry in the UK and his contribution to the development of a polymer acoustic guitar is briefly discussed below.

POLYMER ACOUSTIC GUITARS

There are many reasons not to make polymer acoustic guitars. There is the potential loss of much of the hard won know-how concerning the construction of wooden guitars, the conservatism of guitar players, the strong brand influences that dominate the guitar market and sustainability concerns surrounding the use of 'non-natural' materials. However, the tone woods used for instrument making are in ever-decreasing supply, polymers offer different design opportunities, greater consistency in their properties and affordability. So, it was an interesting case study to explore when research was being conducted into the nature of design knowledge at Loughborough University in the 1990s (Pedgley, 1999). And, as Rob Armstrong pointed out, it is not as if luthiers down the centuries have considered the possibilities offered by woods and polymers and decided that wood was the preferred option!

As I wrote in his citation in 2007 for an Honorary Doctor of Technology Degree at Loughborough University:

'Rob Armstrong started making guitars in Coventry in 1970 where he still works. His understanding of fine instruments is founded on both established traditions and experimental work. Rob works alone. Each instrument is unique, and handmade using basic tools, responding to differences in the properties of the woods. Rob uses seasoned tonewoods – spruce, cedar, pine, mahogany, rosewood, maple, walnut, and ebony. Each guitar has a beautiful, musical sound, and Rob has made over 780 guitars in his 37 guitar-making years. He now aims to complete about 15 commissions a year – leaving time for development and consultancy for Loughborough University.

Rob has made guitars for some of the finest acoustic musicians. George Harrison, Bert Jansch, Gordon Giltrap, Fairport Convention, and the Albion Band. All guitar heroes for my generation. His is an extraordinary talent. In 1989, many of these musicians made a tribute CD entitled *Master Craftsman*. They wrote:

This recording came about because (these) musicians ... believe that Rob Armstrong is one of the finest, if not the finest, craftsmen of instruments in this particular field ...
It is our way of saying thank you Robbie – for making such varied and beautiful instruments ...

His enquiring approach has produced unorthodox instruments including long scale guitars, baby guitars, and double necks ... You may have seen the guitar like a cornflake packet or 'Pudsey Bear', made for Children in Need, or the 'Poppy' guitar for the British Legion. I particularly remember the steel-strung acoustic made from polystyrene packaging, displayed at the Royal Academy in London to some astonishment at Dr Bernard Richardson's lecture.
...

So in 1995, when Loughborough sought to establish methods for making low cost, high quality polymer guitars – an unlikely goal perhaps - we knew where to turn. Rob immediately recognised the design and tonewood conservation opportunities that polymers offered. The project is now a success story and we share with Rob a patent on the new technology. Its many Innovation Awards would not have been won without Rob's knowledge, tireless curiosity and generosity.'

The successful design and development of Loughborough's polymer acoustic guitar is now well documented (eg Pedgey, Norman and Armstrong, 1999; Pedgley and Norman, 2012), but the significant matter to emphasise here is the unique contribution that Rob Armstrong could make. When we discussed a range of polymer samples with Rob he chose polycarbonate as the way forward for the soundboard and explained that it needed to have 'more air in it'. The search was on for suitable foamed polycarbonate sheet and, as they say, the rest is history. 'All-polymer' guitars were exhibited at the Frankfurt MusikMesse in 2002, and Gordon Giltrap made an album – Secret Valentine – using a guitar with a foamed polycarbonate soundboard in 2007. People, including musicians, cannot distinguish between wooden and polymer guitars, and, as might have been anticipated they do not sell because people believe guitars should be made of wood!

However, how was Rob Armstrong able to immediately and unhesitating select polycarbonate and know how it needed to be improved? And it is here we return to Janet Daley. If you have made 700+ guitars, all different, and all successful, your mind has stored patterns and connections that cannot be easily articulated. Guitar makers interact with the materials they use through their eyes, hands and ears and the resulting perceptual data is stored. Rob Armstrong can retrieve this information when he needs to and in response to patterns that he recognises, but that does not mean it is 'describable in linguistic terms'. Perhaps sometime in the future more advanced 'brain scanners' than we currently have access to will be able to analyse the synapses in the brain and decipher memories (if long term potentiation of synapses turns out to be the key mechanism underlying memory), but until then, at least for acoustic guitar design, practical education will be highly significant.

ELECTRIC GUITAR DESIGN: A TRANSITIVE MODE?

Before turning to a more general discussion of design education it is worth noting some differences between acoustic and electric guitar design. Electric guitars are also complex coupled systems, but the electric pick-ups have a strong influence on the sound produced. It is not that the body has no influence on the sound, and in particular, its weight and material will determine the rate of absorption of the energy from the plucked string at different frequencies, but this is to some extent a secondary concern. Very successful electric guitars have been made from recycled tin cans and skateboards, in most shapes and finishes and from most materials, including brass and concrete. So, there is a sense in which electric guitar design reflects Phil Roberts' transitive mode of designing; it is as much about selecting and buying (components) as it is about designing and making. Although anyone can make either an acoustic guitar or an electric guitar, the chances of being satisfied with the quality of the outcome are much greater with the latter.

THE SIGNIFICANCE OF PRACTICAL EDUCATION

Well, it all depends for what! As Sir Christopher Frayling points out in the Foreword it is not sensible to refer to the 'creative industries'. For the antiques trade and museum curation, a practical education might well be seen as unnecessary, although the combination of 'knowing how' and 'knowing that' seems more likely to lead to a secure understanding of 'knowing why'. Dealers in antique musical instruments are much more likely to correctly interpret the alterations that will have been made when strings were switched from 'gut' to nylon. Museum curators will be more likely to categorize instruments in the margins of the guitar and lute families correctly if they understand their construction. So the situation is by no means clear cut, but for creative activities and innovation, it seems inevitable that engagement is necessary with all three kinds of knowledge.

Prior to becoming involved in design education, I was educated as an Engineer. I studied for an undergraduate degree in Engineering Science and Economics and a masters degree in Welding Technology. I was employed as a research engineer at The Welding Institute near Cambridge in the early 1980s and, at that time (it may still be so now), it was the practice for research engineers and welders to work together on the problems that needed to be resolved. It was evident to me then that my understanding of a welded joint was related, but different to that of the welder who had served a 5 year apprenticeship. I knew that as the first weld pass was made in joining a tube – the root pass – that there would be a heat build-up as the welding progressed; that tack welds between the tubes would create local cooling effects; that variations in the fit-up might require changes in the welding parameters and that changes in the material specification could result in defects. The welders knew that as well, but when they made a root pass and you looked inside the tube the penetration of the weld was as specified and of constant width. At that time exactly how the welder achieved this was something of a mystery. Was it the colour of the weld pool? Or the sound of the welding arc that they were responding to? Or perhaps some kind of frictional drag associated with the molten metal? Whatever it was, welders were detecting the need for changes and responding in real time, and they could teach apprentices to do it as well by showing them how. The research engineers were still trying to work out what was happening and programme robots to replicate it. Perhaps they still are. I was well aware of the need for different kinds of knowing and the significance of practical education well before my involvement in design education.

There are other examples that I could give, such as the blowing of large glass vessels for the chemical industry, but however many are recounted here, it will not be possible to generalise from them. From a Popperian perspective they would just be another 'white swan', so, over to Ken and some of his thoughts and recollections.

KEN BAYNES

It might be said that the striking growth of university education since 1960 has overshadowed the importance of other approaches to learning. Apprenticeships and learning on the job definitely appear second best. On the other hand, universities have taken over many subject areas that used to use various models of apprenticeship. Until the 1950s, 'premium apprenticeship' was a respected route into engineering. It often combined very thorough learning on the job with an element of further or higher education. The art schools (set up originally as design schools) provided a formalized version of apprenticeship. Many trades had (and still have) systems of learning on the job with an element of more formal learning. Art and design education have been absorbed into the university sector and it has not always been easy to adapt their essentially practical way of learning to more conventional academic structures. In the ensuing tension it has nearly always been practical learning that has lost out to academic models. This has certainly not been to design education's advantage. Equally it is a pity that universities have not taken the opportunity to examine and recognize the wider advantages of practical learning.

Since universities exercise a powerful influence on schools, particularly the examination system, It is not surprising that schools, with honourable exceptions, also undervalue practical or applied knowledge regarding it as a route for those with a 'different' learning style or, more directly, less able. Of course, the 'less able' may well be academically less able, while having remarkable talents in other areas. It is also the case that these other area might be very valuable for society. Design seems in an intermediate position. Talent in design is valued but, as a subject, its true nature and complexity are not fully recognized. It is also the case that the essential way of learning in design is not fully appreciated and, therefore, ways of assessing it in formal examinations structures are often irrelevant and perverse. The key point is that designing is learnt by designing, not as a professional practitioner but as an active learner. Baynes (2013) recalls his own training at a small art school in north Devon and the Royal College of Art: it was essentially playing the role of the designer and so learning by active engagement with ideas, materials and processes. This was supported by a very useful programme of 'mind-stretching' in the guise of cultural History. It was from such programmes that emerged the extraordinary explosion of creativity that marked British art and design in the decades after 1960.

Practical education is, in fact, much older than academic education. Records of it go back to the first cities and it seems certain that hunter-gatherers and early farmers learnt on the job. We have particularly good accounts of medieval education (Shahar,1990). Guilds were very important in towns but both aristocrats and peasants often learnt by being attached to a family. By the Renaissance (Burke, 1972) academies provided courses in medicine, theology and the new humanism but the Guilds and families were still the dominant medium for learning. Burke records, for example, the extraordinary network of family ties and apprenticeships that linked architects, engineers and artists. Going into the family business was clearly a very common career choice. A key point with the Guilds, which continues to be important in the design professions, is the idea of a master PIECE rather than a master's THESIS. Ability to do replaces the ability to research and analyze. This is entirely logical. We do want an architect or doctor or engineer to be capable of delivering the goods, we do not mind so much about his or her theoretical knowledge. Of course, the essence is the interaction between theory and practice but in the design professions theory is an enabling tool giving the designer either greater certainty or a way into a design situation.

The time has come to look again at the model of apprenticeship and recognize its value in both general and practical education.

It is startling how little contact children now have with practical making. As a result their making skills are often rudimentary. Skills and applied knowledge are not learnt at home or taught at school. This has been well-documented in the case of cooking but applies equally to other 'basics' such as handling scissors of using glue (Brochocka and Baynes, 2013). The only way to learn these skills is to practice them and primary school teachers report that there is now little time in the curriculum for 'practice'. Yet practice is the essence of competent performance whether it is in sport, reading, throwing a pot or designing. The idea of mastery has an important place in primary education, not in the sense of professionalism but in the sense of a skill or idea 'mastered' sufficiently for the pupil to be able to use it flexibly and confidently. Picking up on the notion of modelling, we might say that a 'model' - in this case how to do something - has been mastered and is now ready for use. Such mastery is liberating. It not only widens a child's field of action but also opens up new thoughts and new ways of thinking about the future.

A further factor in children's lack of practical awareness is the almost complete lack of observable practical work in the day to day environment. Except perhaps for house building and highway maintenance, most things are now conceived, made and mended behind closed doors. Even the school kitchen is likely to be out of bounds or supplied with dishes prepared and cooked off-site. Mum may cook at home and Dad may do DIY (or vice versa) but quite frequently they are simply too busy to welcome help. This was not the case in the past. Even in the 1950s there were many small enterprises with open front doors and people usually cooked at home. Such availability gave young people a perspective on practical making and was a source of inspiration to future design professionals. For example, in 'Giants of Steam' Jonathan Glancey (2012) describes the childhood experiences of Oliver Bullied who grew up to become the Chief Mechanical Engineer of the Southern Railway during the Second World War. Before that he had worked with Nigel Gresley - designer of 'Mallard' the world-record holder for steam speed - at Doncaster. As a child he lived in a remote corner of Wales:

> 'Oliver was fascinated ... with craftsmanship and the making of things. His village of Llanfyllin in mid-Wales boasted a blacksmith as well as a cooper, a coppersmith, and a tinsmith. Oliver helped them all. And if he was not in the smithy, he would find something useful to do in the local sawmill or gasworks. Here was a child with his head in the clouds of imagination but with his feet firmly on the ground.'

Such a formative experience would not be possible today. Although children now have access to extraordinary sources of information and (second-hand) experience, it must lack the immediacy and reality of Bullied's village. It won't do to romanticize the past. No doubt the young engineer- to-be also witnessed at first-hand grinding poverty and hard labour in the fields, but the skilled trades on his doorstep were a vivid inspiration. It is worth wondering what schools, museums, art galleries, businesses, universities and the design professions could do to open up practical 'designerly' experiences to young people.

3. ENCOURAGING THE IMAGINATION ... *Ken Baynes*

Designing calls for the use of many different skills and many different types of knowledge. Imagination is indispensable. Imagination is essential because design is only called for if the future is unknown. If we already know what we need to know, there is no necessity for design activity though many crafts, cooking for example, involve 'designerly' thinking to organise and plan the work.

Imagination is also essential in order to understand and evaluate design proposals. It is a common experience to find that potential users of a product or environment cannot extrapolate from drawings, models or computer programs to imagine what the finished result will be like in reality. Yet this is a skill that is essential both in organising life at home and exercising democratic rights over large scale planning decisions.

Children's cognitive development has been much studied. Their imaginative development has been comparatively neglected. The importance of play is accepted as an essential part of growing up and it is recognised that playing requires the ability to imagine and pretend. However, imagining and pretending are not given the dignity they deserve though both are fundamental to human creativity. Equally, the changes to the world of imagination that happen at puberty have not been seen as an educational opportunity though the heady mix of idealism and despair produces radical flights of the imagination. Both childhood fantasy and teen-age rebellion are of potential interest to design education because they engage with the forms of things unknown.

If I was looking for a dynamic growth point in design education it would be in the interweaving of childhood and adolescent imagining with adult experience. The learning potential on both sides of this equation could be very great.

We need a lot more research on the imagination and how it can be fostered by teaching and learning. Here is an area where Design and Technology should take a lead and in conjunction with other subjects join with psychologists and cognitive scientists to tackle an important research agenda.

- What happens in the mind when the imagination is in action?
- How do mental and physical models and modelling media support the imagination?
- What is the connection between imaginings which are pure fantasy and those directed to shaping future reality?
- What are the developmental stages in the emergence and growth of imagination and how do these relate to other areas of intelligence?
- What teaching and learning methods are effective in fostering the imagination, in general and specifically in relation to designing and understanding design?
- Is it possible to evaluate pupils' imaginative development?

ENCOURAGING THE IMAGINATION

Stephanie Atkinson

Albert Einstein once famously said that the true sign of intelligence is not knowledge, but imagination (Viereck, 1929). Imagination, as the basis of creative activity, is an important component of all aspects of cultural life, enabling artistic, scientific, and technical creation alike. Every invention, whether large or small, before being implemented and embodied in reality, has been held together by imagination (Vygotsky, 2004). Imaginative thinking sometimes referred to as 'possibility thinking', helps drive innovation in technology at organisations such as Apple, Google and NASA (Warren, 2011). Imagination also plays a role in social identity and meaning making, as a cognitive faculty by which individuals and groups make sense of the world (Norman, 2000). Having a novel idea, finding something valuable in some way in an idea, or making something out of an idea, all require having imagination to frame possibilities.

Imagination is a highly complex gift that we all possess and one which must be encouraged. Many writers have likened it to a muscle that you cannot see or feel, but which is very much there, with the suggestion that like a muscle it must be exercised and strengthened or it will waste away. Vygotsky (2004) talks about the brain that not only stores and retrieves past experiences, but also combines and creatively reworks elements of those experiences in order to generate new proposals and new behaviour, and that this is imagination. He refers to two types of experience. One type is more often referred to than the other. The first type depends directly on the richness and variety of a person's own experiences. The richer the experience is the richer the material is that the imagination has access to. The second type occurs when the experiences of one person are described to others thus broadening their experiences and enabling them to imagine something they have not actually witnessed themselves.

Pelaprat & Cole (2011) define the process of imagination as the process of resolving and connecting the fragmented, poorly co-ordinated experience of the world so as to bring about a stable image of the world. Gardner's (2007) definition of imagination suggests that it is the ability to see the unseen before it happens and NACCCE[2] (1999) in the same vein states that it is principally to do with seeing new, or other possibilities. In terms of using imagination, Law (2007) suggests that it is the process of supporting and generating original ideas, providing an alternative to the expected, the conventional, or the routine.

Craft (2002) proposes that there are three aspects of imagination: imaging, imagining and being imaginative. She explains that imaging and imagining are both essentially mental processes. She suggests that imaging can take on a variety of forms such as visual, olfactory, auditory, or gustatory forms and she, and many others, believe that it usually involves memory of something that already exists. She also indicates that when imaging is shared that imagination can be developed. In explaining the uniqueness of imagining she proposes that it involves intention,

---

2 National Advisory Committee on Creativity and Cultural Education (NACCCE)

supposing or entertaining a hypothesis, and that imagining as well as including the use of memory can in certain contexts involve 'pretending'. The third element of imagination Craft explains is 'being imaginative' which may not necessarily be purely a mental act. She uses such terms as *'going beyond the obvious', 'seeing more than is initially apparent'* or *'interpreting something in a way that is unusual'* (Craft, 2002, p 81) to describe imagination. She suggests that one can visualise without being imaginative, one can be imaginative without visually imaging and one can both visualise and be imaginative at the same time. However to say that someone has been imaginative, Craft (2002) and others indicate that it must involve some kind of outcome as well as incorporating mental processes.

Any discussion concerning imagination cannot avoid including reference to the closely related subject of creativity. Vygotsky (2004) characterises creativity as a process that arises from imagination. He also states that creativity is present, not only when great historical works are created but also whenever anyone imagines, combines, alters, or creates something new, no matter how insignificant the new outcome appears to be, when compared to the inventions of geniuses.

The importance of the role of knowledge in developing imagination is also well researched. Knowledge is what you already know; imagination is what makes it grow. Even genius inventors cannot create in a vacuum (Ochse, 1990). As Craft (2002) explained:

> 'If a child is to identify possibilities, or exercise imagination in any context, this must be done with knowledge, for without it a child cannot logically go beyond what is 'given'.' (p 30)

Closely associated with, but distinct from being imaginative is fantasy. Fantasy should not be considered the opposite of memory. However it does depend upon memories, which it utilizes in new ways and combinations (Vygotsky, 2004). The terms 'fantasy' and 'imagination' when used to describe activities in everyday life, tend to be associated with things that are based on reality, and at times even aspects that are not actually true. As such, in the context of everyday life, it is sometimes not taken seriously or considered to have any practical significance. As already explained being fanciful lacks objectivity or direction and yet much research has rightfully insisted that fantasy play should be encouraged, particularly for young children, as it has been shown to correlate with other positive attributes that children need to develop (Taylor et al, 2004). Young children have a natural ability for using their imagination and often use fantasy to great effect in their play and pretend games. The research of Taylor et al (2009) indicates that those with imaginary friends are more creative, have greater social insight and therefore are better at understanding other peoples' perspective. Craft (2002, p.18) suggests that although these flights of fantasy do not bear any resemblance to serious creative activity, they are in fact *'the seeds'* that grow into creative abilities, provided the right *'fertilizer'* is added. Neilson (2012) and others agree with Craft (2000) when she proposes that imaginations' origins are in the imaginative play that children engage in from very early in life. He suggests that imitation and pretend play are critical developmental domains in the evolution of *'human cumulative culture'* (p.172). Fundamental to our progression as a species is our capacity for invention.

Our ability to think creatively sets us apart. As stated above being imaginative doesn't just appear when we are adults, nor does it all develop at once. It slowly evolves from more elementary and simpler forms into more complex ones and its development depends on other types of human activity, especially the acquisition of knowledge and experience (Vygotsky, 2004).

Children are hard wired to be imaginative. Imagination is innate, it cannot be lost but it does require nurturing. During a child's early development, research has demonstrated that parents who talk to their children regularly explaining such features as, nature and social issues, or those who read or tell stories at bedtime, seem to be most likely to foster pretend play and therefore imagination in their children (Singer & Singer 2005). An early educational environment in which pretend games are encouraged has also been shown to lead to greater amounts of imaginativeness and enhanced curiosity (Ashiabi, 2007; Singer and Lythcott 2004).

The important concept of 'theory of mind', an awareness that one's thoughts may differ from those of other people and that there are a variety of perspectives of which each child is capable, are closely related to imaginative play (Singer and Singer, 2005; Jenkins and Astington, 2000). So in terms of education, both formal and informal, space needs to be provided to allow this to happen.

On the opposite side of the coin is the proven fact that as well as being imaginative it is human instinct to learn by imitation. Bartel (2009) suggests that schools, parents and society do much to condition children to be spectators rather than active strategic game players, and that once established this situation often continues into adulthood and becomes more difficult to overcome. In his condemnation of this state of affairs he goes on to suggest that when education is seen as merely producing experts to imitate experts there is a failure to foster the majority of human potential.

In explaining imitating and imagining Bartel (2009) makes reference to 'Mirror Neurons' and 'Imagination Neurons' to be found in the brain. 'Mirror Neurons' cause us to imitate without the need to think. Although this is acceptable for some dexterity skills, and one must remember that not every task calls for innovation, we do not learn how to learn to think by using our 'Mirror Neurons'. It is our 'Imagination Neurons' that allow us to be imaginative and these neurons only grow if they are used.

As changes in the world accelerate, society requires fewer imitators and more innovators to survive and succeed; therefore it is important that our educational system provides the opportunities for pupils to 'grow' their 'Imagination Neurons'. Innovations require critical thinking about aesthetics, philosophy and ethics. The prerequisite to this is the cultivation of divergent thinking during childhood. Thinking that can imagine what has not yet existed, and this is in no way through imitation of what already exists.

For years, imagination was just thought of as a way for young children to escape from reality, and that once they reached a certain age; it was believed they would leave fantasy behind in order to deal with the real world. However over recent decades child-development experts have recognized the importance of imagination and the role it plays in allowing young children to form their understanding of reality (Wang, 2009). Open-ended play encourages a highly individual experience that is fuelled by imagination. It opens the doors to independence, self-confidence and unlimited potential (Emmenegger, 2012). Through play, children can express the world they visualise inside themselves and begin to understand the outside world that surrounds them.

There has been much concern raised over the fact that as children grow up they become less able to use their imagination (Craft, 2002). This is considered a natural consequence of children maturing and becoming constrained by social convention. There is considerable evidence to suggest that the way in which children are educated impinges greatly upon this aspect of their development. The role of the teacher is vital. Teachers must take every opportunity to foster imagination and promote curiosity. Children naturally wish to please those in authority. In a school situation they therefore want to provide correct answers to problems they are set in order to receive the praise that such answers will accrue. At a certain stage in their development children will begin to avoid presenting new, untried solutions which they are unsure of, as these they believe may not meet with their teacher's approval and therefore make them feel stupid or childish. Assessment regimes that are used in educational settings tend to support this requirement for 'the' correct answer. It would appear from educational researchers and psychologists that children of today are playing less and using their imagination less (e.g. Singer & Singer, 2005). Although Russ (2003) in a longitudinal study found that children's use of imagination in play and their overall comfort and engagement with play activities has actually increased over the 23 years and 14 studies that she conducted. She believes that our busy technology world has not retarded children's imaginative capabilities. She uses analysis of her results to show that children who exhibit good play skills in both imagination and emotional play situations show better skills at coping, creating and problem solving.

Children's curiosity needs to be encouraged and supported through the provision of toys that make children curious; toys that can satisfy their questions about how things work. Various studies blame the proliferation of television and electronic toys such as video/computer games for the decline in play (e.g. Singer & Singer, 2005). While the appropriation and transformation of adult objects into child playthings is nothing new with children having their own versions of, for instance: weapons, prams and tools, the high level of technology incorporated into child-friendly electronic gadgets is new. This type of toy does not require the child to use or develop their imagination; rather children are utilizing someone else's imagination. Simple toys first designed in the past are generally in a form where the child can work out their function, thus developing skills that will support future imaginative thinking. Whereas electronic toys work as if by magic and cannot be understood nor do their workings need to be understood in order to play with them successfully. Emmenegger (2012) specifies that using such toys to promote social acceptance and positive self-esteem encourages conformity and a lack of imaginative activity.

NACCE (1999) indicates that many children lose their natural power of imagination once they are faced with the formal structure of schooling; and that most never regain this ability. Much research has been carried out to try to explain other reasons for this drop in divergent thinking (Bartel, 2010).

The role of adults in improving children's imaginative skills with positive consequences on their creative abilities is also well researched. In particular the role of teachers during early schooling in providing the optimum balance between structure and freedom of expression has been shown to be particularly fruitful. The implication for education is that if we want to build a relatively strong foundation for a child's developing imagination, then what teachers and parents must do is to broaden the experiences that are provided for them.

It is the balance between developing a sound knowledge base and at the same time allowing imagination to flourish that causes many teachers a problem, and the fact that this becomes even more problematic the older the child becomes. Much research has been carried out into the problems associated with continuing to develop a child's imagination, as they grow older. There are numerous reports to be found in the literature and on the World Wide Web. However, the majority are concerned with identifying the problems and very few on how to overcome them.

The importance of pupils being provided with appropriate props and freedom to choose what to use in imaginative play have both been shown to be important in encouraging imagination. There is a need to make space in the curriculum both conceptually and physically for being imaginative, for imagination grows best with new experiences and lots of time and space to explore. Being imaginative requires motivation. It may not necessarily be willed but it is not to say that it is without intention. Being imaginative is not accidental and may require concentrated activity to achieve.

Encouraging imagination in the early years of a child's education is relatively straightforward, as imaginative play forms a crucial part of every primary teachers' toolbox of teaching strategies, although recently the concerns over poor numeracy and literacy skills have squeezed the time that can be given to creative aspects of the curriculum. Those opposed to the narrowing of the curriculum have explained that although learning multiplication tables and the alphabet are important that memorising does not teach children to think or be imaginative (Emmenegger, 2012).

The importance of role models in terms of parents, teachers and even older pupils who model that being imaginative is a good thing and lots of fun has been well researched. Such children have a better chance of developing into interesting curious, creative, imaginative children as they grow up. Suggestions for supporting imagination in the literature are many and varied. These include encouraging real experiences and observations, ones not from imitations, using visual stimuli both in the classroom and outside by visiting art galleries and museums, and even providing children with magnifying glasses to observe the world around them from a different perspective. Observation is said to be the mother of imagination.

The more experience, the greater the imagination that can be brought to bear on potential solutions. Although Boden (2001) does indicate that there are no guarantees on how to foster 'imaginative activity' Haskvitz (2006) makes several suggestions for improving the development of imaginative thinking in a classroom context. He believes that it is the most overlooked aspect of a child's education. Indicating that schools tend to *"...stuff children full of facts without bowing to the greater good of creativity and the encouragement of imagination".* He talks about the importance of enabling children to be imaginative as it allows them to take up the position of decision maker in a way that is perhaps not normally available to them. He also suggests that certain classroom activities are better at encouraging imaginative thinking than others and explains that teachers must not be overly didactic or prescriptive, they must actively encourage play and experimentation with new ideas. Boden (2001) supports this belief when he explains that in order for imagination to flourish there needs to be less structure and focus on skill building and more on just having fun although he does support the belief that using Science and Mathematics can provoke a pupil's imagination.

During a child's education many teachers and even parents become too focused on trying to teach children concrete memory based concepts. Thinking outside the box tends to be discouraged. In fact when it comes to secondary education imagination is given little if any value. In today's secondary curriculum children tend to be commanded to "Stop dreaming", "Act your age", and "Do as I tell you" (Callahan, 1992) and yet, encouraging the continued development of imaginative skills is vital to both the young adults' continuing development and the wellbeing of society.

In terms of the problems faced by teachers themselves, there are such aspects as the difficulties associated with fostering divergence, difference, and individuality while at the same time managing a large class of pupils. This can be particularly problematic for the teacher when the curriculum is to some or even a large extent specified by others. There is also the dilemma associated with a teacher's need to plan how they can make pupils aware of novel possibilities if they themselves are unimaginative or are unaware of the possibilities available. It is also the case that many teachers who need to feel in control tend to spend little time with their pupils exploring unexpected ideas when they are unsure of the direction that the idea might take the pupil. Many teachers believe that it is their responsibility to be able to foresee and plan solutions to every problem almost before it arises. It is essential that teachers develop the ability to be content with shared uncertainty. This is a skill that is prevalent in those who are naturally creative. They need to develop the ability to do things differently; to change their habits of work, for a true enemy of imagination is acceptance of the status quo.

The role that teamwork can play in encouraging imagination cannot be underestimated. Sharing thoughts and bouncing ideas between pupils and between pupils and their teacher can be an excellent means of developing imagination. To do this successfully all parties must feel at ease with sharing their ill formed ideas. Research findings also indicated that when people are relaxed they are much more likely to have those big 'eureka' moments, those moments of insight where seemingly impossible problems are solved.

Children who are encouraged to use their imagination and not be judged either way by the outcome have a better chance of continuing to hone this skill throughout their education. Unfortunately, as children learn more they learn the realities of life, for instance a spoon is for mixing and isn't a doll's head or part of a musical instrument, and this has been shown to inhibit their ability to use their imagination.

Children need to be given open-ended problems to solve, ones that avoid stereotyping.

A teacher's empathetic stance is essential in allowing them to provide tasks that are challenging, of interest to pupils and yet not too difficult for their abilities thus avoiding frustration. The greatest gift to give children is for them not to be afraid to use their imagination. Teachers need to foster experimentation, play and divergent searches for ideas. Pupils need to be encouraged to be choice-makers by allowing them to make decisions. Unfortunately choice can sometimes lead to disappointment when the outcome fails to work out. Teachers and pupils must be able to celebrate mistakes as learning, and remember the 'serendipity' effect, as many important discoveries begin as mistakes. Teachers need to break the habit of seeing imagination as only appropriate for art or music. They need to encourage the process more than the product and enable pupils to use all their senses, which will make them more aware of all the possibilities.

Assessment is often held up as a problematic area when tasks that involve creativity and imagination need to be assessed. Assessment can drive teaching and learning strategies and discourage divergent thinking, and yet assessment and accountability are aspects of education that will not go away. When group-work is being used as a teaching strategy, and as already discussed working in teams to solve problems helps develop imagination, assessment can become a major stumbling block. One solution is to use such assessment criteria as: listening ability; tolerance for diverse ideas; ability to contribute unusual ideas; ability to see and find good questions; ability to encourage and seek ideas from those who are not contributing; ability to summarise and synthesise well. These can all be assessed both as peer assessment and teacher assessment and can provide vital feedback that can encourage imagination.

Keeping an open mind is difficult in a world where one-word answers are the key to a good test score. As a community teachers therefore need to develop strategies that allow assessment to take place, but in a manner that will not inhibit imagination. Using a variety of assessment methods is one way that can provide the space for imagination to flourish. One teaching strategy that promotes imagination is the use of questions, as questions can promote thinking. However in terms of the questions to ask it is important that they are not questions that only have a right or wrong answer as this can suppress imagination that requires space for the unexpected, novel or divergent thought.

As well as providing positive ways forward to encourage imagination there are a number of 'do not' statements that if avoided will remove some of the imagination inhibitors. In terms of evaluating imagination, care should be taken not to tell learners whether imagined solutions are good or bad, or why an idea will or will not work, instead ask them to explain their ideas. This will help the teacher access the mindset of the pupils. In the same vein one should not overly reward imagination, as there is a tendency for that to cause a loss in the desire to improve an idea. In terms of questioning, encourage the use of open/ thinking questions. Stimulate pupils with replies that ask them for further insight, questions such as 'what would happen if'; 'What do you think?', 'Is there a better way?' and 'try it and see'. Questioning of this nature will push the child's imagination and allows ownership of the idea/thought to remain with the pupil. Teachers should be careful how they give praise. To tell a pupil that an idea is excellent can make the child think that only this one answer is required. Instead use praise in terms of 'I like the way you used your imagination to answer that'.

CONCLUSION

Imagination, as the basis of creative activity, is an important component of all aspects of cultural life, enabling artistic, scientific, and technical creation. It is therefore vital that imagination is encouraged at every stage of a child's education. Being able to use one's imagination depends upon the acquisition of a broad knowledge base and as rich a variety of experiences as possible, ones that can be utilized in new ways and combinations. Young children naturally use their imagination in their games and pretend play to great effect. However, once children are faced with the formal structuring of school they seem to loose that ability and most never regain it as they progress through the educational system. It would appear that there are two main reasons for this. Firstly it is considered a natural consequence of children maturing and becoming constrained by social convention. Secondly there is considerable evidence to suggest that the way in which children are educated impinges greatly upon this aspect of their development. In order to alleviate these problems teachers need to take every opportunity to achieve a balance between developing pupils' sound knowledge base and at the same time allowing imagination and curiosity to flourish throughout the educational system and not just when children are very young. The difficulties identified with assessment regimes imposed upon older children can be alleviated if teachers change their habits of work; develop their own skills in coping with shared uncertainty; allow children to be in the position of decision maker and develop teaching strategies and questioning strategies that will support and encourage imagination.

4. THE COGNITIVE VALUE OF AESTHETIC AWARENESS ... *Ken Baynes*

Aesthetics are wrongly identified with surface appearance, the icing on the design cake. Alternatively, they are wrongly identified with expression, an emotional gesture or personal hallmark. In fact, aesthetics are fundamental to all human thought and action, and particularly in designing and making.

All human cognition depends on input from the senses. The big brain's causal models are built from sensory input. Action in and on the world is carried out though the senses and it is feedback from the senses that leads us to modify our actions and to learn from experience. Seeing in the mind's eye relies on models constructed from sensory experience and these models are externalised and understood through sensory output and input.

Humans live in an environment, natural or made, of shapes, forms, colours, movements, actions and reactions. It is these sensory, aesthetic qualities which are the basic 'stuff' of designerly thinking just as words are the basic 'stuff' of linguistic thinking.

People have strong reactions to their surroundings. A place can be disturbing or reassuring, for example. These perceived qualities come partly from 'wired in' reactions that are the result of evolution and partly from cultural values that vary from place to place and from time to time. Our aesthetic 'intelligence' partly determines the thoughts we have and the actions we take.

Aesthetic judgements are not 'just a matter of taste'. Uninformed taste is not taste. The truth is that humans have created a formidable body of knowledge about aesthetics and the way people respond to the made world. Take, for example, the mathematical basis of pattern, proportion and form. Historical cultures, East and West, have explored and documented the underlying harmonies that are evident to humans. Designers have used their insights sometimes without knowing the theory. The key reason for studying design history is to be able to read the aesthetic handbook represented by the products of the past.

Aesthetics are central not only to designed things but to the way we communicate them through models. Fluency in the use of aesthetic media contributes directly both to the clarity with which a designer can externalise design ideas and the efficiency with which they can be shared by other people.

At Loughborough we have been exploring the idea of 'graphicacy' as an important element in the curriculum. Research suggests that this is a further area for cross-curriculum development. The cognitive value of drawing and computer graphics, for example, links the arts with the sciences. The ability to read and interpret graphic images is essential in everyday life as well as many trades and professions. Design and Technology and Art and Design could take the lead in this area by joining with others to revisit and re-define the role of aesthetic awareness and graphicacy in the school curriculum.

THE COGNITIVE VALUE OF AESTHETIC AWARENESS

Krysia Brochocka and Ken Baynes

In Western Europe there is a long history of aesthetic discovery and analysis. An understanding of scale, proportion and space are evident in classical Greek buildings, ceramics and sculpture while Greek philosophers and mathematicians set down a number of fundamental geometrical propositions which still underpin practical aesthetics. Other early civilizations, particularly Japan, China and India looked at aesthetic qualities from philosophical, artistic and religious viewpoints. Much of the craft and architecture of these cultures demonstrates an approach to design in which aesthetics and fine workmanship are prime values.

The first surviving written work to link aesthetics and design is around 2000 years old but the author, Vitruvius, was able to refer to other, older works now lost (McKay, 1978). Vitruvius was an architect/engineer with a practice in Augustan Rome. His 10 books on architecture – De Architectura – cover technology, technique, professional standards, architectural education, modelling systems and the aesthetics of building both to serve a function and to give pleasure. His work continues to influence building design even today. Translated by Brunelleschi (1377 – 1446) it was a handbook for Renaissance artists and architects who sought links with the classical past to help them forge a new humanist style of building. Taken up by Palladio and set out in magisterial detail in his books on architecture, the resulting Baroque style with its carefully considered system of proportions related to the human scale first conquered Europe, then every corner of the world where European culture came to dominate.

In the eighteenth century there was a meeting of minds between designers, artists and scientists. The Enlightenment saw mathematics as a key to human knowledge and there was keen interest in extending both the boundaries of mathematics and linking it to buildings and other structures. In the industrial revolution there emerged a new 'industrial aesthetic' which delighted in pure form. Engineers identified with solid geometry and its representation in engineering drawings. These drawings were the visual language of industry and in a real sense made possible the revolutionary machines that wrought dramatic changes in the everyday lives of working people. Writing in 1863, James Nasmyth, inventor of the steam hammer (Baynes and Pugh, 1981) precisely identified the fundamental aesthetic values that underpinned the industrialized world of the nineteenth century:

> 'Viewed abstractly the forms of the various details of which every machine is composed, we shall find that they consist of certain combinations of six primitive or elementary geometrical figures, namely, the line, the plane, the circle, the cylinder, the cone, and the sphere; and that, however complex the arrangement, and vast the number of parts of which a machine consists, we shall find that all may be as it were decomposed and classed under these six forms; and that, in short, every machine , whatever its purpose, simply consists of a combination of these forms, more or less complex, for the attainment of certain objects and performance of required duties.'

For Nasmyth there was an almost magical significance in solid geometry.

The twentieth century became an aesthetic battleground as the modernists, such as Walter Gropius and Le Corbusier called for a rejection of all traditional styles. They wanted an architecture fit for a revolutionary age of mass culture and industrialization. As Reyner Banham (1960) showed so clearly, the result was itself a style. The apparent purity of modernism collided with consumerism after 1950 and, from then on, aesthetic qualities became partly defined by their ability to sell goods. With exceptional foresight, Marshall McCluhan saw the relationship between lifestyles, advertising, the media and product aesthetics.

Modern theories of aesthetic qualities as makers of meaning were first set out by Gyorgy Kepés, Rudolf Arnheim, E H Gombrich and Herbert Read. These looked at aesthetic qualities from the perspective of art but recognized their significance for the more day-to-day concerns of design. In 'Education through Art', Read (1943) presented a complete programme for general education in which art practice and aesthetics would be the key elements. The book was influential, leading to the establishment of an international organization to pursue its aims. However, if its effect on art teaching was substantial and for the good, the more general idea of learning widely through the medium of art was never accepted in any state education systems. An exception may be Venezuela where La Systema brings music education to everyone, not simply for its own sake but also for its positive influence on the mental and social development of young people.

Today there is considerable evidence as to the cognitive value of aesthetic awareness from evolutionary biologists and neuroscientists. For example, Ellen Dissanayake (1992) argues that art and aesthetic understanding played a key role in creating human meaning for early humans. She sees aesthetic qualities as being essential to the productive and ceremonial activities of *homo sapiens sapiens* because they have the capacity to 'make special'. It certainly seems that every made object that has survived from the earliest times is finished more beautifully (and often decorated) to an extent not needed for its utilitarian purpose. This is an early emergence of the two-fold function of design activity: to do a job but also to do it in such a way that satisfies the human desire for beauty and meaning. E O Wilson (2012) traces human aesthetic sensibilities back to the experience of hunter-gatherers. They had to have a keen ability to read the signs presented by the environment and these were in the form of sensory information. It was vital to attach meaning to these signs. Wilson even suggests that our present aesthetic preferences are still formed by our early experiences in Africa:

> 'The habitation innately preferred by people has had a considerable impact on landscape architecture. Believed by many researchers to have originated during prehuman evolution in the African savanna forest, the predilection includes dwelling on a height that is near a body of water and looks down on fruitful parkland (with large animals in sight, even if only represented by sculpture).'

This is a perfect description of the landscapes created in the eighteenth and nineteenth centuries by Capabilty Brown and Humphrey Repton for wealthy landowners.

Neuroscientists have focused on the role of aesthetic qualities in shaping the causal models that are constructed by the human mind and the way these determine what we think. Steven Pinker (1998) identifies cognitive models as being essential to the success of *homo sapiens sapiens* because they enable humans to respond flexibly to changing situations. The models have a particular significance for design activity because they are the medium in which design thinking takes place. It is by modelling the future, in the mind and then in such externalized models as plans and drawings, that the imagination is given form. The mind only has access to the external world through the senses. It is from sensory information that the causal models are built. They are not 'neutral'. Although the brain is fundamentally the same in all people, each brain is shaped by its own life experiences. The brain is constantly attempting to match new information with previous experience and previous experience is also shaping the new information!

Neuroscientists acknowledge that there is still much to be learned about the interaction between sensory information and the mind, particularly consciousness and our mental models. Physiologists wonder if there are 'building blocks' in the brain which have specific receptive fields (Zeki,1999) and how this might relate to, for example, human appreciation of art or even personal tastes in clothes or products. What does seem to be certain is that certain defined areas of the brain are specialized in processing specific sensory information and that these are closely related to the well-established areas of aesthetic enquiry – in the case of vision, colour, pattern, space, movement and facial recognition. So aesthetic awareness is essential to human thought and indeed survival as well as being fundamental to design.

AESTHETICS AND DESIGN

Aesthetic qualities are fundamental to design because they provide the 'language of form' for the construction of mental models, externalized models and the resulting environments, systems, products and communications. They are also the language which allows users of design and commentators on design to give meaning to their views and reactions.

Design is concerned with creating a made environment which serves the needs of humans. It is axiomatic that humans shape their environment and are in turn shaped by it. This is a dynamic relationship, constantly changing in response to new technologies, beliefs and information.

Design activity crosses the barriers between the humanities and sciences, using concepts and knowledge from both fields. This is because all made things must exist in the physical world but must also satisfy human needs that are spiritual and psychological as well as physical. Aesthetic qualities form a bridge between these two realms of knowledge and understanding.

Aesthetic qualities could be related to or derived from, for example, sociology or mathematics. Sociology could provide insights into the aesthetic preferences of a particular group of people; mathematics could be the key to developing a modular system of proportions for the design of an exhibition panel system.

Although aesthetic qualities might often seem to be part of a design 'problem', they are also an important source of solutions and creative approaches.

FORM

Design proposals are realized in the real world when ideas and speculations (modelled in the mind) are translated into physical forms. In the design field these are traditionally identified as 'shape, line, colour, texture' etc, but these are principally visual/spatial concepts that need to be supplemented to give a comprehensive picture. In fact, most physical forms that result from design activity will have implications, however slight, for all the senses. On occasion a particular sense will dominate the design activity. Structural design of the ceiling at Snape Maltings was primarily for the purpose of achieving good acoustics. It also had structural integrity and provided a special visual/spatial setting for the audience. Design is multi-facetted precisely because human requirements are multi-facetted.

The form of things is best seen through the lens of the relationship between people and their environment. Not surprisingly, this is a relationship that has been much studied in different ways by artists, scientists and people in the humanities. It is from the visual arts and architecture that 'shape, line, colour, texture' originally come. Science has added to these qualitative labels knowledge of perception, environmental psychology, anthropometrics and ergonomics. These add quantitative data and explanation to qualitative responses. Novelists and poets have explored the affective nature of the link between people and places and their experience of the made world. There is no shortage of knowledge but there is a tendency to neglect or 'not notice' the richest store house of knowledge and experience, immediately available to everyone, which is the places, products and communications that have already been created.

In design activity, the resulting form comes from the resolution of factors that are likely to be in conflict. For example, human needs, available materials and techniques, cost and timescale. The weight given to each of these factors is a matter for decision on the part of the designer and it is clear that these decisions will determine the form that the designer creates.

In his classic book, *The Nature of Design*, David Pye (1964) provides a good discussion of this situation:

> '... the shape of all designed things is the product of arbitrary choice. If you vary the terms of your compromise – say, more speed, more heat, less safety, more discomfort, lower first cost – then you vary the shape of the thing de-signed. It is quite impossible for any design to be 'the logical outcome of the requirements' simply because, the requirements being in conflict, their logical outcome is an impossibility ...'

> 'The whole art of planning is compromise.'

Of course, some compromises are more effective than others and it is up to the designer to get the most out of the requirements.

CONCEPTS CONNECTED WITH FORM

Form – the physical configuration of a natural or designed entity – has been studied from many different perspectives. Below is a selection of concepts that seem to have special relevance for design activity or understanding design. They are far from exhaustive but give an indication of some approaches to aesthetic awareness that could be valuable in education.

1 The form of the made world influences human behaviour and serves human needs through the medium of all the senses: sight; hearing; taste; touch; and smell. Each of these has a related group of concepts, knowledge and experience in the humanities and science as well as design.

2 In order to communicate in design, one must have a 'language' of form and in this instance it is shared with art. The formal qualities they share are: line, shape, form, pattern and texture, light and colour, rhythm and movement, space, proportion and scale, harmony and dissonance. This group of concepts is more than just a means of communication, it is also the basis of aesthetic understanding. This basic list can be supplemented by others. For example: dot; line; shape; value or tone; balance; harmony; and dissonance.

These can be further analyzed for each quality. They can also be combined. The SHAPE of a MOVEMENT could be: straight; curved; zig-zag; random or free-form; spiralling; twisting; winding; rotating; encircling; rolling; hugging; hovering; fanning; weaving.

All such concepts are hard to model or represent in words, they require a visual model for full understanding.

3 Designers have adopted a number of values about the form of environments, products and communications. They underlie much of the structure of the made world. Since they are not always compatible with each other, it would be impossible to act on all of them at the same time. In fact, many encapsulate a particular design ideology.

Emulating the natural world in the made world. Using the forms of animals and plants as an aesthetic 'reference book' or as a source of technological innovation - frequently both.

Truth to materials. Materials are believed to have intrinsic aesthetic qualities which should be respected. Many of these values have their origins in centuries of handwork.

Form as an expression of function. The purpose of an object or environment should be evident in its appearance. Aesthetic qualities are believed to emerge from 'solving the problem' rationally. This concept underpins much engineering design and was a tenet of the modern movement in architecture.

Form and spaces should relate to the scale and capabilities of human beings.

Form as a means of expressing symbolic values – the soaring vaults of a cathedral reaching towards heaven or the American roadside cafe in the form of a doughnut.

Efficiency: using the least resources necessary to reach a given result. Often linked with form follows function.

The potential of technology. The idea that any given technology can result in a particularly perfect expression of its functional efficiency – a racing car for example or clothing for survival.

Design can reflect the culture and 'spirit of the times'. Fashion and style are powerful influences. Most obviously in clothing, graphics and consumer goods but some would argue in ALL designed things.

Design builds on previous traditions. What already exists is a storehouse of examples of aesthetic ideas and design solutions.

There should be a coherent 'language of form' throughout any made things.

4 Many areas of design have their own particular set of concepts with aesthetic implications. For example, approaches to making buildings more socially 'responsive' and to provide a richer social and visual environment:

Robustness – buildings and places should be adaptable.

Richness – designed to appeal to all the senses.

Personalization – allowing and encouraging people to make them their own.

Permeability – a variety of building shapes and routes and a mixture of public and private spaces.

Legibility – meaning that the plan of a place should be evident and that the form of a building should have symbolic value.

5 In developing a design idea, it may be useful to adopt different starting points. Often the choice will have aesthetic consequences. Examples include:

Analysis of user's needs (including their tastes and cultural background).

Exploring the potential of forms and structure.

Beginning from an understanding of the qualities and potential of materials and/or technologies.

Being in tune with style and fashion, working with the 'spirit of the times' (or deliberately reacting against it).

Starting from the ordering capacity of modules and proportional systems.

Understanding the cultural values of a particular market

AESTHETICS AND DESIGN EDUCATION

Learning about art, design and making are important childhood experiences that are influenced by general physical, intellectual and emotional development and, in turn, contribute to it. At all ages art and design experiences have a special role to play in the development of aesthetic awareness, imagination, observation and practical making skills.

It used to be thought that children were like empty vessels waiting to be filled with knowledge, morality and skills. This included aesthetic awareness and an appreciation of beauty. It has now been proven that in order to survive babies have to interact with the world around them. Evolution has programmed them to learn and, equally importantly, to want to learn. Curiosity is wired-in. From the moment they are born babies are learning and developing. They acquire new skills simply by being alive in a social setting and they acquire them at an astonishing rate. For example they learn: to coordinate their movements; to see; to grasp; to respond to others; and to get their own way.

All of these contain the seeds of other kinds of understanding. For example, moving, seeing, grasping and interacting with others are all fundamental to aesthetic awareness.

Development is partly pre-programmed, partly the result of environment. Each individual has a unique genetic inheritance but the way it plays out depends on the process of growing up, cultural background and education.

Aesthetic education and design education are interlocked. Designing and understanding design depend partly on aesthetic awareness. At the same time design activity and studying design contribute to aesthetic awareness. In design the learning medium is active - learning through doing. To design it is necessary to become visually literate. One must learn and practise a non-verbal language. Although seeing begins automatically, it can and must be continually developed and taught.

Awareness and curiosity are perhaps the key words. The aim is for the student to be open and alert to aesthetic qualities, to recognize them in the environment and use them creatively in design activity. This was well summed up by Bruce Archer in one of his Royal College of Art papers:

> ' ... the arousing of curiosity in the natural and man-made (sic) worlds. The discovery of how things look, feel, work and behave. It is the becoming aware of underlying fundamental principles and qualities, the inter-relationship between them, their inseparability ... in the forming of the intrinsic nature of a natural form or artefact, PROPORTION, STRUCTURE, FUNCTION, the inter-slotting and sliding of parts, mechanics, control and then further values (such as) colour, tonality, surface quality, the appreciation of materials and technical concepts and the balance between the emotional, intellectual and aesthetic.'

5. THE VALUE OF LEARNING THROUGH MAKING ... *Ken Baynes*

Primary teachers have a distinguished record of understanding the pedagogical value of 'learning through doing'. It provides a vivid and absorbing way into many areas of knowledge. In recent years 'learning through doing' has become less common throughout all sectors of education. Worse still, one particularly valuable expression of 'learning through doing' has suffered acutely. This is 'learning through making'. Cost, time and social attitudes have all contributed but the end result is an unbalanced curriculum offering, the loss of a brilliant strategy for learning and the impoverishment of children's school experience.

By learning through making, I mean something rather more than the production of images and objects that has traditionally been a central element in art and craft education. In my view, it is essential for children to have such experiences, but here I am casting the net a little more widely.

The issue was clarified for me many years ago when looking at work by seven and eight year olds at Severn Beach Primary School near Bristol. Rather than simply write poems or stories (again, essential activities in their own right) the children had made simple 'miniature books'. These were enchanting objects in themselves and a source of great pride and satisfaction to their creators. More importantly they had involved the children in a wider world of skills and decision making:

- The books had to be planned
- The relationship between words and pictures had to be thought out
- There was a purposeful process to creating the text: rough drafts; editing; final draft; word processing; proof reading
- There was a similar purposeful process to making the illustrations
- The whole had to be brought together in a series of page layouts within the limitations of producing an 8, 12 or 16 page book from folded sheets
- The resulting book was shared with others and the class had a lively discussion about the difficulties and pleasures of authorship, editing, illustrating, graphic design and book production
- The class had enhanced their skills, their self-esteem and their confidence.

You could say that this was a design and make project and certainly the children had designed and made their books. However, the work put graphic design activity into the context of the wider world of books and the broad range of activities necessary to bring a book into existence.

My point is that we need to make the best possible educational use of the fact that we are involved with making. Making has revolutionary educational potential.

LEARNING THROUGH MAKING

Gill Hope

In Primary schooling in England in recent years, an increasingly academicised curriculum has devalued the worth of practical hands–on activity. Although teachers are aware of children's different learning styles and of Howard Gardner's work on multiple intelligences, there is nevertheless an implicit hierarchy that places those intelligences related to reading, writing and mathematics ahead of others, including music, artistic and practical capabilities. Three ways of learning are commonly recognised: Visual, Auditory and Kinaesthetic (under the acronym VAK). The requirement that children listen well to their teacher and recognise and decode visual elements in presentation of information (texts) means that children who are struggling with academic skills are assumed, thereby, to be the "kinaesthetic learners" (poor things). The truth of the matter, however, is that we are all kinaesthetic learners and that this is the primary pathway whereby babies, toddlers and young children learn about the world. Babies watch and listen, but they also reach out and grasp. They clutch and shake and rattle and put things to their mouths. Toddlers poke things with sticks, kick at balls and run. Young children push carts, ride bikes, squidge play-dough, run sand through their fingers. Then they arrive in school. In the Early Years, they are encouraged to continue to develop these essential encounters with the real world, but all too soon schooling becomes pencil and paper and a whiteboard. Those who can listen, see and write are advantaged over those who learn in other ways; and the essential learning through doing is lost to everyone. Children who have little practical experience of the wider world are doubly disadvantaged; how can you write of sea and sand if you have never felt or smelt the sea or run across the sand and discovered the pools among the rocks?

By providing practical hands-on experiences in school, teachers can in some measure make up for these disadvantages. Children can talk (and later write) about the experiences they are having now, in the classroom. They can find and learn words for the feel and smell and potential of materials that they are handling and using. They can understand the layout of a Saxon village so much better by building one from recycled boxes with lolly stick fences than by looking at a picture or watching a video. Such learning by making engages the learner in several ways. Firstly, they have to consider the real 3-dimensional layout and relationship between the parts, the sizes, shapes and negative spaces between the elements. Secondly, they have to physically construct the parts, developing flexibility and strength of the hands, co-ordinated with the eye, learning to use simple tools, finding out how to join materials effectively, whilst holding in mind how the finished product should look. Thirdly, they are engaged emotionally in the task, not just in terms of their own satisfaction of the doing and the making but in entering empathetically into the lives of the people who once lived in such a village: Where would they keep their cow? Who would be the blacksmith? Why was a church built on the hill? Such depth of reflective questioning surfaces so much more readily through active making than through passive watching and listening.

Primary school teachers have, of course, always known this but recent pressures on time, the over-crowded curriculum, the spectre of basic skills testing has led to an increasingly unbalanced curriculum to which such deep learning has fallen victim. And the deepest, hands-on learning of all is becoming increasingly rare within many, many schools. By this I mean designing through making, especially within the context of Design and Technology.

I do not mean that children are not encouraged to be imaginative. Many good teachers are inspiring and creative practitioners and pupil results are impressive – but often in an increasingly narrow range of skills; sadly, only those needed for the tests. The range and depth of the curriculum has suffered in response to these pressures and, not surprisingly, those schools whose children come from homes with greater social capital tend to do better than those whose children come from families less able to provide a rich and stimulating home life. In terms of educational entitlement, the narrowed curriculum is adding to the disadvantage of many of our most vulnerable young people.

By learning through making, children see the picture they have in their mind's eye become something real and tangible. By designing through making, they can see their own ideas come to fruition. This is powerful. This is worth learning in its own right. This goes through citizenship (seeing themselves as able to make a difference in the world) through history (appreciating how people's decisions and choices have shaped the world we live in) to understanding industrial and political geography, to moral, spiritual and religious education, to understanding the need for social justice and political engagement. Or would we rather have an apathetic, consumerist society who have been taught to be disengaged by becomingly increasingly passive learners? Perhaps some would. Personally, I would prefer that not to be the legacy of my lifetime of working in education.

Those are big claims, are they not? Let us unpick the skills and attitudes that underpin learning through making and see if such big claims be justified.

In Parkinson's (2012) research into young children playing with construction kits, he identified the skills of manipulating, modelling, mending and modifying in all situations of children's making (which he dubbed the 5 M's to make them memorable to trainee teachers). These skills were not just happening physically but also cognitively, in the mind's eye. As the children manipulated the pieces of the kit, trying out the various ways in which those pieces might fit together to make something resembling the picture in their mind, so that inner image was also being manipulated. Pieces were being fitted together with the hands, but the visual image was being rotated within the mind or imagined with another piece added, a different piece placed, maybe with a quick glance at what someone else was doing and imagining how their friend's idea would fit with their own. Being able to hold, feel and manipulate with the fingers was so integral with the thinking mind that often the attention did not seem to be with the fingers at all, because the sense of touch was informing a part of the brain that freed the eyes to search for new solutions. The whole brain was working in consort as the making progressed.

What was happening inside the brain was the constant modelling and re-modelling of ideas, in conjunction with the modelling and re-modelling of the developing product being made from the kit (Roberts, 1992). My own research (Hope, 2002) into young children of 6-8 years old using drawing for designing, tracked several potential pathways for the developing model. Sometimes a child had one good strong idea, which they recorded, perhaps tweaked a little, and then went on to make. Sometimes they could see several alternative solutions and would make a series of quick sketches and might either choose one to develop in the materials provided or reject all their drawn ideas because the drawing had helped clarify what would not work. As they became older and more confident and capable in using drawing to develop design ideas, the children could put on hold the need to try out their ideas immediately in the real materials and manipulate these on paper through further drawings (Hope, 2005). However, this could not happen without rich prior experiences with real materials and also without a depth of discussion with peers about their ideas as they developed.

This parallelled Parkinson's (2012) mending and modifying that he observed with children using construction kits. Ideas that did not work were changed. Ideas that were unrealistic were scrapped. Good ideas that came apart when discussed with friends were fixed, often with a bit of social glue as well as real glue as the ideas became transformed into real products. The modelling and manipulating of ideas through talk, the 'what you could do is ...' comment or the 'I can't quite ...' appeal for help, pushes children into a level of dialogue and depth of articulation of thought that does not, at this young age, come out of a discussion of a mathematical calculation or the writing of a descriptive text.

The articulation of inner imagery and half-formed thoughts within the real context of making can thus positively enhance children's language skills and their ability to put their inner thoughts and ideas into words. This was borne out by Stables and Rogers' (2001) research into developing language skills through Design and Technology. Both boys' and girls' language skills were enhanced across the duration of the project, including punctuation and spelling. This suggests that the imperative to express oneself clearly and the need to employ standard conventions for doing so is focussed and transformed into reality through the context of a real task and the need to communicate concisely and effectively.

Applying such analogues (drawing, mock-ups, discussion) to a future outcome that can be tested in the real world requires more skills: estimating one's own capability with tools and materials (could I do that?); assessing materials & their potential (will that make that?); planning ahead and confronting problems of communication and resources. The projection of ideas into the future and considering possible outcomes, which are then evaluated and modified as they are evaluated against task requirements and success criteria require children to imagine products and solutions that do not yet exist. Prior knowledge and experience will undoubtedly inform the ideas and procedures invoked in the current project but the application of such knowledge, skills and understandings into the practical making of a product reinforces, deepens and extends all three. The application of knowledge in a new and different context, that of practical making, allows children to see how that knowledge works within the real world.

For instance, a child might see a picture of a pulley system in a book but until they have hands-on experience of assembling such a system, they can have no real appreciation of the real power advantage of the pulley. The hands-on experience is also more likely to be remembered (Harrison,1978).

However, in designing Technology there is another layer: the user and the purpose. The user may also be implicit in model-making in other subjects. For instance, in History (there was a miller owning and running the windmill; the tepee needs a door and a smoke hole) but the needs of the user are not always made explicit to the children. Attaching a set of card sails to a recycled plastic pot with a split pin does not enable the children to get to grips with how the technology actually worked and what it did. Experimenting with plastic gears, pulleys and wheels would actually allow children to understand and appreciate the technology as well as engaging them in imagining real solutions to the problem of harnessing the wind to grind the corn.

It is only with the support of real materials or components that children can embark on thinking through and coming to an understanding of the relationship between elements of technological systems, their inherent possibilities, potentials and limitations, and addressing problems in which specific criteria are assigned or embedded. Indeed, this is impossible for adults without some degree of knowledge of a technology and how component parts might work. For instance, many of the people who stand on canal banks watching the lock gates open have little idea of the hidden mechanisms below the water line that allow the gates to be opened or even of the precise fitting of the gates within the shoulders of the lock sides which utilises the weight of the water itself to prevent it from escaping down the hill. In the past 250 years, since the beginning of the Industrial Revolution, the British countryside has been transformed through the construction of such canals - and then of railways, trunk roads and airports, pylons and substations, wind farms and solar panels, radio masts and satellite dishes and the myriad satellites now orbiting beyond the edges of earth's atmosphere, plus the out-of-sight systems below ground of cables, oil lines, gas pipes, sewers and optical fibres; all this underpinning the supply and demand of contemporary technological lifestyles and a globalised economy. In order to begin to make sense of this complex world in which they live their lives, children need to undertake real tasks with real components that allow them to make and model real technological solutions.

Many of the products made by Primary aged children are, strictly speaking, models rather than workable products, being largely made of paper and card rather than the materials of the real world (Hope, 2006). For instance, children might be asked to design and build fairground rides combining basic consumables such as paper and card with recycled materials such as CDs (carousel bases), egg boxes (cut up to make seats on rides) or rolled up newspaper for structures such as roller-coasters. This making of a model requires the skill of seeing "as if" in which children excel and which adults frequently overlook as simply playing, that is, making one thing stand for another. For instance, a large cardboard box might be a house one day, a ship the next and a garage tomorrow. However, this analogical, metaphorical skill of reading one thing as if it were another is foundational to all higher thought and is a uniquely human capability. No other species on the planet can do it, even in maturity; yet human children think this way instinctively and all learning is built on it. The small child's inventive re-use of the cardboard box is little different to the fashion designer's re-combination of retro styling with contemporary fabrics.

The skills that the fashion designer uses in construction of a garment, as well as imagination and flair, are a deep understanding of the drape and handle of fabrics that can only come from practical hands-on experience. The subtle ways in which different fabrics hang and move with the body cannot be simulated by computer graphics alone, especially if they have surface sheen, slubs or stretch. Patterning, texture and colours radically change the way the garment appears to fit the body or enhance the cut of the garment. This kind of knowledge comes from real experience not theoretical knowledge. If the British economy is to continue to benefit from the exports of the design industry, the children in Primary schools today need to be equipped with those hands-on skills through practical activity and through making real products.

It could also be argued that as the economy continues to fail to expand that being able to make things for oneself rather than buying ready-made will be increasingly important for many people to maintain a good quality of life. The high turnover of DIY outlets suggests that many adults currently have the practical skills to fix simple plumbing and electrical problems for themselves, build furniture from flat-packs and decorate their homes. Such levels of personal independence need to be maintained within the population through teaching children practical skills that can be built on later. Confidence in one area of handiwork frequently begets a willingness to attempt related skills in other fields.

Another, related argument for skilling the population with practical know-how is the wider issue of finite global resources. A throw-away society in which new goods are constantly imported from developing economies on the other side of the world is not sustainable, economically or morally. The cleaner environment of the post-industrial UK is at the expense of someone else's pollution in a poorer part of the world. If children were taught to make things for themselves, especially from recycled or reclaimed resources, this would contribute to lessening the global carbon footprint of humanity. Learning to make things for oneself teaches not only the process itself but also to value the hours spent by others in producing the wares in our shops. An understanding of how long it takes to make something may also encourage children to realise how little these producers must get paid and thus to begin to question the principles on which the global economy is run.

The proliferation of ready-meals and easy availability of high calorie snacks in UK supermarkets and other food outlets has been causing concern within government departments for some years, triggering initiatives for teaching cookery to children in schools. This has been a commendable strategy which should continue to be supported and indeed extended through specific funding. By learning how to prepare and enjoy healthy foods, to feel the sense of satisfaction in feeding oneself creatively from raw ingredients, children are being taught that eating a healthy diet is possible and pleasurable. Some schools also have gardening plots in which children can grow their own vegetables, fruits and salads. This should be encouraged as children need to understand where food comes from and how it is produced. One area of technology that has always been missing from the UK National Curricula from design and technology is agro-technology, which other countries, such as Malaysia, include (Kementarian Pendidikan Malaysia, quoted in Hope et al., 2011). Our farms and fisheries supply us with high quality food through the application of modern technology. Children need to be taught about this, but through practical activity not just through books and videos – and their practical action needs to be more than simply watering a pot plant and feeding the class goldfish.

It might be argued that understanding the science that has enabled these developments would be sufficient. However, This does not allow for the thinking through of the implications. One might quote here the application of Rutherford's understanding of the structure of the atom to the construction of the atomic bomb only a few decades later. Technological education should also include the human element and learning this through making a product for a specific user provides children with a groundpoint from which to consider such ethical issues. Working together on a common project that will result in a viable product requires the employment of valuable skills of collaboration and negotiation, of listening to others and anticipating their actions. It demands a growing respect for the creativity, capabilities and viewpoints of other people and an appreciation that there is a range of possible workable solutions to the same problem.

Unlike science, which seeks to find overarching unified theories to explain universal phenomena, technology seeks to combine and apply knowledge from fields as diverse as physics, art and social psychology to solving a particular problem in the here-and-now (Buchanan, 1996). By constructing real solutions to a problem arising from a specific human need, children engage in the reality of materials science, the aesthetics of product appeal and the social psychology of human wants and physical needs. This may be through making a model of something a story character might want (a coach for Cinderella) or an individual with whom they can empathise (a pop-up card to send to a friend in hospital) or even something they might want themselves (attractive Easter egg packaging). Through providing a balanced range of such situations to consider, the teacher can offer children the opportunity to use their own developing practical skills and capabilities to address real human needs.

When engaged in such practical action, in making a real product, children are engaged in a purposeful process that is goal oriented whose outcome can be tested in the real world against the initial task criteria. The child's thought process becomes public through the success of the product, but what also becomes viewable is the range of solutions that can satisfy the same criteria. Children learn to evaluate their own thoughts and accomplishments against the achievement of a viable solution to a complex problem of the kind that Rittel and Webber (1969) identified as 'wicked problems' those socio-technological situations for which there is no simple right or wrong answer. Middleton (2000) called the area inhabited by such solutions as the 'satisficing zone'. This class of problems are indeterminate: solutions are best-fits given the state of present knowledge and capability. Dealing successfully with such ambiguity of problem and outcome is high-level thinking, especially when required to produce a real product that actually works.

Admiration for each other's creativity and expertise in so doing contributes to a shared pride that develops children's self-confidence and, claim Davies et al (2001) a form of spirituality. The completed work, on display in the classroom, evokes a shared sense of pride and appreciation of one another's creative capacities. It is also evident that many children really enjoy such practical making and become utterly engrossed in the process. Csikszentmihalyi (1988) called this being in a state of creative flow in which time almost stands still as total absorption takes over. Barnes (2007) links this to well-being through neuroscientific evidence of endomorphines in the brain that are activated by engagement in creative action. He also quotes international evidence that school-aged children in the UK are well below those in other countries on measures of well-being and personal happiness. Might this be due to the pressure of learning too much factual information and not enough time to process and apply what they know in a creative environment? Barnes certainly thinks so.

But does this not sound like an argument for the arts? For music, dance, painting and drawing? Do Primary children really need to get involved in the complexities of making things for someone else and that really work? Is this not for older children? Better left until Secondary school?

One of the reasons for introducing Design and Technology into the Primary curriculum in the 1988 Education Act was that Secondary teachers believed that higher standards could be achieved if children began to study the subject in Primary schools. Previously, Primary schools had done Art and Craft which involved making things but not necessarily tailored to a user and a purpose, or model making that did not closely represent how the object worked. The successful introduction of Design and Technology to the Primary curriculum (DfEE/QCA ,1990) resoundingly demonstrated that not only are Primary-aged children capable of thinking in these ways but thoroughly enjoy doing so. Its introduction was an act of faith, written by people with virtually no experience of working with Primary-aged pupils but with sufficient insight into their subject to be able to extrapolate downwards to create a working document. Quickly revised (DfEE/QCA, 1993) and simplified it evolved into the confident statement of 1999: that the subject involved evaluation of familiar products, focussed practical tasks to gain necessary skills, and design and make assignments to allow children to engage deeply and fully in creating their own products to satisfy a design brief relating to a specified user and purpose (DfEE/QCA, 1999).

If this subject were to disappear or be reduced to being a handmaiden to other subjects, then the depth of thinking required in grappling with real problems could be lost. Making a card model of a Tudor house might be a way of keeping children happily occupied whilst improving their cutting and colouring skills but it pales in comparison to thinking about being one of the Pilgrim Fathers setting off across the Atlantic and having to build a house on arrival. The children would need to research what a house meant to those people, where they slept and worked to grow, store and cook their food, washed themselves and their clothes, or manufactured and repaired tools, furniture and wagons. With this depth of knowledge, building a model of a house, let alone a village becomes an intellectual challenge, a real problem that would develop children's empathy, understanding and intelligence. This would be doing real history as well as engaging in real designing and making. If a cross-curricular model of Primary education of this depth and sophistication could be devised, then this would develop children's minds alongside their practical skills.

If language studies ("Literacy") were removed from its separated slot on the timetable and integrated within the rest of the curriculum, children could develop literacy in context. They could write letters home from Plymouth, MA to Plymouth UK containing annotated diagrams of their farm and lists of resources they needed to be sent on the next ship. The reply could include the bill and instructions on how to make a chair or some other piece of household furniture. These instructions could be tested through making, and so on. By immersing themselves in the construction of a whole scenario, children's learning would be holistic and meaningful. Practical action would be integrated with intellectual activity. They would have learnt about people, not just as a group who lived a long time ago, but as people facing situations with which they could identify and through the role play of making models enter into their experience and understand how it was to be them.

Thus I would argue for a fully integrated curriculum for Primary school children, with opportunities to engage in practical making as a full part of the entitlement of that curriculum. I have indicated some of the outcomes of recent research into the skills involved in making products, unpicked the wider intellectual gains of involvement in practical work, examined the contribution of Design and Technology to the Primary curriculum, and suggested how this way of regarding practical activity not only informs children about the made world but enables them to be empowered through planning and making their own design ideas and solutions to real human needs and wants. Such activities are not simply low level hand skills (cutting, shaping, joining) but offer real intellectual challenge to our ablest pupils whilst developing the all round capabilities of all children in our Primary schools.

6. THE CREATIVE RELATIONSHIP BETWEEN DESIGNING AND MAKING
... *Ken Baynes*

The National Curriculum has always presented the relationship between designing and making in a particularly unhelpful way: one before the other. It is true, of course, that there is a sequence of events in designing and making that moves towards an end result. However, the rigid stages imagined in the National Curriculum might have been carefully designed to stifle creativity.

I will summarise some of the negative effects:

- The assumption that the making simply carried out the design. In reality, making will throw up problems and possibilities that can change the original design for the better and make it more practical and realistic

- The assumption that most designing will be drawings or digital media. In reality, making in the form of 3D-models, test-pieces, lash-ups, colour tests and other 'roughs' is a way of designing

- The assumption that what is made must be a fully realised product. In reality, this limits the areas of design which pupils can experience. This requirement has led to environmental design being largely excluded even though it is of fundamental importance

- The assumption that what is made must be the result of a lengthy design process. In reality, this is not universally appropriate. Food is a good example. The requirement has led to trivial design work that has detracted from a number of important areas of craft skill

- The assumption that all designerly work should begin from an identified need, problem or brief. This has tended to stereotype the nature of design activity. From an educational perspective it is enriching to have projects of varying length and with a variety of starting points. In reality, design can start from a particular material, a technological innovation or an aesthetic insight. It can start from playing around and trying things out.

In summary, designing and making need to be reunited. Sometimes making can be free, expressive and experimental. At others it needs to be directed towards a prescribed goal. In either case, designerly thinking can permeate the process. Designing becomes a state of mind, an innovative attitude to the whole of designing and making rather than a stage in the process.

THE CREATIVE RELATIONSHIP BETWEEN DESIGNING AND MAKING

Eddie Norman, then Niall Seery

'There is nothing more practical than a good theory.' (Lewin, 1952)

Lewin made this statement in the context of social science over 60 years ago and it has been a much used quotation and provided an excellent point of departure for numerous papers in the intervening years, as it has once more. Except this time, although it is not perhaps a logical corollary, there is a need to look at a parallel position.

There is nothing so debilitating as a bad theory.

Lewin's message was that theorists should strive to make sense of the real world and that practitioners should endeavour to make use of theoretical positions. The proposition of the existence of 'a/the design process' is a theory, but is it 'practical' or 'debilitating'? Ken Baynes has noted some of the negative outcomes of this proposition, and particularly those that derive from the separation of designing and making if, as an aspect of this 'design process', they become to be seen as sequential activities. Can they really be separated? Before returning to this discussion, it is useful to review some evidence.

'MAKING' IN INDUSTRIAL DESIGN

One of the outcomes of a PhD research project by Eujin Pei (2009) was a taxonomy of the modelling methods employed by industrial designers. These were initially coded on 114 playing cards, which were then adapted into a 'more portable and accessible format to support the education and practice of designers at all levels' (Evans, Pei and Campbell, 2010) . In this simplified format, there are 32 cards, categorised in four sections: sketches, drawings, models and prototypes. The cards were placed in one of four sections in which that particular modelling approach had been found: concept design, design development, embodiment design and detail design. The cards also indicated the types of design and technical information being addressed, but these matters lie outside the scope of this paper. These would, of course, be an important source of understanding concerning the appropriate use of different modelling methods in this particular design area, but the current concern is the matter of separating 'designing' and 'making'. So, to this end, these 32 modelling methods are shown listed in the design phase in which they were found in Table 2.

It is evident that both 2D and 3D modelling methods were found in the design development, embodiment and detail design phases and it was only in concept design that the modelling methods used were solely 2D. It should not be assumed that the methods shown in italics represent making 'by hand'. It is clear from the photographs shown that many of these 3D modelling methods involved the use of CADCAM either for the entire outcome, or components of it, although clearly there is likely to have been 'hand finishing'. So, whatever the hoped for separation between 'designing' and 'making', there is no evidence for it here. The evidence could be taken to suggest a difference between 'concept design' and the other design phases in that the modelling methods found for concept design were 2D only.

This evidence also suggests that the analysis of appropriate modelling methods is quite complex even within this one design area. If further evidence were presented in relation to other design areas, such as fashion, graphics, furniture, engineering, architectural, landscape, interiors, transport, urban design and town planning, this complexity would only increase. So it seems apparent that from this direction of enquiry that the separation of 'designing' and 'making' is at least a poor theory.

TABLE 2 TYPES OF MODELLING METHODS USED IN DIFFERENT PHASES OF INDUSTRIAL DESIGN (based on Evans, Pei and Campbell, 2010)

2D > plain text, *3D > italics*

Design Phase	Modelling methods
Concept Design	Idea sketch, Study sketch, Referential sketch, Memory sketch
Design Development	Coded sketch, Information sketch, Sketch rendering, Prescriptive sketch, Scenario & Storyboard, Layout rendering, Presentation rendering, Diagram, Perspective drawing, *Sketch model, Design development model, Functional model, Operational model, Experimental prototype, Alpha prototype*
Embodiment Design	General arrangement drawing, Technical illustration, *Appearance model, Assembly model, Production model, Service model, Beta prototype, System prototype*
Detail Design	Detail drawing, *Final hardware prototype, Off-tool component, Appearance prototype, Pre-production prototype*

However, perhaps there could be some evidence that 'concept design' always only involves 2D modelling methods, which might lend some support. So, for evidence relating to this possibility let's turn to the work of Jeff Conklin at the CogNexus Institute.

OPPORTUNITY DRIVEN PROBLEM SOLVING

In discussing the nature of problem solving Conklin (2006) refers to a study in the 1980s at the Microelectronics and Computer Technology Corporation. This study examined the behaviour of experienced and expert integrated-circuit designers, as they worked on elevator systems, an area that was new to them. Each participant was asked to 'think out loud' as they worked on the problem, and the resulting videotapes were analysed. The analysis showed that these designers worked simultaneously on understanding the problem and formulating a solution.

'On the solution side, their activities were classified into high, medium and low levels of design with high-level design being general ideas, and low being details at the implementation level. These levels are analogous to an architect's sketch, working drawings, and a detailed blueprint and materials list for a house.'   (ibid, p. 4)

The expectation was that these designers would proceed through a process analogous to the 'waterfall model': gather data > analyse data > formulate solution > implement solution: an all too familiar expectation.

'However, the subjects in the elevator experiment did not follow a waterfall. They would start by trying to understand the problem, but they would jump into formulating potential solutions. Then they would jump back up to refining their understanding of the problem. Rather than being orderly and linear, the line plotting the course of their thinking looks more like a seismograph for a major earthquake … We will refer to this jagged-line pattern as opportunity-driven, because in each moment the designers are seeking the best opportunity for progress toward a solution.'   (ibid, p.5)

And later …

'In particular, the experiment showed that faced with a novel and complex problem, human beings do not simply start by gathering and analysing data about the problem. Cognition does not naturally form a pure and abstract understanding of 'the problem.'   (ibid, p.5)

'… another striking observation: problem understanding continues to evolve until the very end of the experiment. Even late in the experiments the designer subjects returned to problem understanding… Our experience in observing individuals and groups working on design and planning problems is that, indeed, their understanding of the problem continues to evolve – forever!'

There is no suggestion in this study that 'concept design' only takes place at the start of the design activity, but there still might be a credible distinction that, when it does, it always takes place using 2D-modelling, although this might also be 'clutching at straws'. And the participants here were expert designers, not children. So, perhaps children behave differently? Malcolm Welch's research has provided evidence on this from which we can draw.

CHILDREN DESIGNING

In 1997 Welch reported the results of analysing the design protocols (audio and video recordings) for 5 pairs of Year 7 students in Canada. The students were asked to construct the tallest possible tower using one sheet of white paper and clear tape. They were also given pink paper to use as they wished during their design activity, but it could not be part of the outcome.

'Analysis made evident five significant differences between modelling as described in the literature and as used by subjects. First, three-dimensional modelling largely replaced two-dimensional modelling. Second, subjects developed solutions serially rather than producing several solutions at the outset. Third, three-dimensional modelling was used to manifest not only existing ideas but to fuel new ideas. Fourth, modelling was used to develop and also to refine ideas. Fifth, models were evaluated not only upon completion but from the moment that designing and making began. These results suggest it is important to provide students, early in the process of designing and making, an opportunity to explore, develop and communicate their design proposals by modelling ideas in three-dimensional form.'   (Welch. 1997, p61)

And as Welch noted:

'Subjects in this study used three-dimensional modelling in a number of ways: to increase understanding of the problem; to externalise a cognitive model; to transform a two-dimensional model into a three-dimensional form; to fuel ideas for further cognitive modelling …The bulk of students' untutored technological problem-solving skill will have been acquired in the material world: building sand castles, using commercial construction kits, constructing with found materials, and so on.'   (ibid., p64)

However there was a significant concern at the time that these behaviours might have been the result of the students having insufficient 2D-modelling skills to represent their ideas. So in 1999 Welch reported the results of working with a colleague to repeat the study after the children had had specific teaching inputs concerning sketching. This was the conclusion.

'Throughout designing and making sketching is used for a variety of purposes. Initially, sketches may help to explicate needs, define and clarify the task. Later they are used when exploring ideas, evaluating proposals, identifying design problems and communicating with others. Sketching may also encourage the development of a general design ability.

The study reported here has shown how, when left to their own devices, Year 7 novice designers, whether taught sketching skills or not, do not use it as a way to develop a proposal. Rather, students explore their mental images using three-dimensional materials. Subjects in this and earlier studies did not view sketching as a mediating instrument between mind and hand. Yet if students are to develop capability in designing and making they must learn the relationship between sketching and thinking, and how to use sketches to clarify and show details of their design thinking.'   (Welch. 1999, p193)

So there really is every reason to believe that theoretical models that separate designing and making as separate aspects of 'a/the design process' really are bad theories. Niall Seery now develops the some of the implications of this position.

NIALL SEERY

DESIGN AND MAKING: NATURAL ENQUIRY

Building a tent at the back of the sofa, acquiring additional height to access the cookie jar, dressing up to embody an imaginary persona, devising a plan to stay up late and creating the biggest and most extravagant sandcastle are all examples of natural behaviours that young people navigate through designerly thinking and realisation. The importance of the making helps refine these ideas and is the catalyst for further enquiry. Most of us can relate to these and similar activities from our youth or observing young people and qualify the distinct relationship and intertwining between designing and making. The educational value of design and technology is in the natural synergy between designing and making.

In the young person's world, these creative design activities are spontaneous, unstructured, and iterative, modifications are immediately executed and evaluated, and often the end product is incomplete, yet supports their imaginative vision and application. In their world there is no misconception that designing is a defined processes (either in structure or duration) and there is no misconception that the make must be fully realised. Instead the quilt slipping off the back of the sofa will often result in more ingenious methods of stabilising/modifying/ of fundamentally redesigning the structure. The norm in this activity is enquiry, explorations, and experimentation, limited only by the strength of their convictions. There are no rules, obligations or restrictions. Imagine if the norm and practice was that these designs must be fully realised, designer behaviour must have followed a defined prescribed path and could only be executed once the design was finalised? It would be difficult to comprehend the effect this would have on these naturally inquisitive activities.

Bridging the gap between natural human capacity and efficient and effective designerly thinking is fundamental to the argument of how we support young people developing and externalising their innate imaginative and creative capacities. Fish (1990) suggests that scaffolds such as words, pictures and models as imitations of objects, scenes or events not physically present, significantly increases the pupils ability to engage in mental visualisation. Seeing in the mind's eye and understanding the relationship between the design and designing allows for external representations that can be utilised as a medium of reflexive conversation between the designer and the brief (Kim et.al. 2009) as a 'sense making activity' (Kimbell 2004). The PhD works of Diarmaid Lane (2011) further emphasis the relationship between developed externalising skills and enhanced creative capacities. In his research with Initial Technology Teacher Education students, he presented not only a model for developing realisation and modelling proficiency, but also highlighted the impact this capacity has on building mental imagery and synthesising skills.

DIFFERENT THEORETICAL POSITIONS

There are various theoretical positions that could be considered when navigating the complex space of design and technology education. As the learning process is often predicated on students' ideas and the outcomes generally divergent, the emphasis must focus on the process of constructing meaning.

Taking a general view of how students perceive, input, process and comprehend information will give some insight into the significance of the relationship between having ideas and developing the ideas into coherent evidence of learning. Felder and Soloman developed the Index of Learning Styles (Felder and Spurlin, 2005), an instrument to assess learning preferences within four dichotomous cognitive domains, their work acknowledged that effective learning should aim to achieve 'balance' within each domain. Even by taking a cursory look at the learning characteristics defined in Table 3, the potential of design education to achieve balance is clear.

TABLE 3 FELDER SOLOMAN INDEX OF LEARNING STYLES DICHOTOMOUS DOMAINS

Dichotomous Domains	Learning Characteristic
Perception	Sensing/Intuitive
Input	Visual/Verbal
Processing	Active/Reflective
Comprehension	Sequential/Global

However, separating designing and making immediately skews Felder's idea of balance. Viewing the purpose of making as an activity to carry out a design propagates a sequential approach to designing. Synthesising ideas/information/ forms etc more globally is critical to design thinking, where the focus is on building the mental imagery in the absence of physical reality. Processing this imagery and idea(s) is best refined by the iterative relationship between thinking and doing. We process information by acting and reflecting on it. Kolb's (1984) experimental learning cycle encapsulates the relationship between planning, doing, reviewing, and concluding and forms the basis for the international consensus on what is effective experiential learning. Dow (2006, p. 309) subscribes to this position and advocates the move from the transmission of facts or the demonstration of skills to the development of active, autonomous learners and encourages the active participation of the learner in authentic and meaningful learning experiences.

'NEED TO KNOW' VERSUS 'HAVE TO KNOW'

If you consider the behaviours of learners and the process of learning, then the relationship between making and designing is significant in supporting creative enquiry. Maintaining the assumption that making simply carries out the design, is particularly unhelpful and serves to define a narrow view of what is expected of the student, valuing maladaptive function over more adaptive behaviours.

The uncertainty embodied in design based activities can be used to support students developing more enquiring habits. Design tasks once supported can shift the paradigm from one of 'have to know' to 'need to know', as students not only create their own solutions but often their own problems. The approach stimulates an adaptive process of enquiry and experimentation leading to the development of a broad and relevant knowledge base in the subject area.

Based on a longitudinal study Canty (2012) has shown that the act of integrating a design based approach in the development of craft and processing skills had a significant influence on student engagement in the learning process and the development of subject knowledge and skills. He attributes increased attainment to the needs created through the iterative process of designing. The personalised nature of the design activity served as a catalyst that pushed the students to their limits as they decided how best to represent and realise an idea that was unique and personal to them through their mastery of craft and processing skills. Canty (2012) furthermore illustrates how experimentation, trying things with unsure outcomes and learning from mistakes were valued above all by students during the design based learning experience. For these students the essential construction and transferability of new knowledge and skills fostered a deep learning experience, where disciplinary and transdisciplinary knowledge and skills were accessed and developed as required.

Similarly, Claxton (2008) describes his approach to 'Building learning power' based on what he defines as Resilience, Resourcefulness, Reflectiveness, and Reciprocity. This theoretical position is supported by Gerver (2010) who like Canty (2012) focuses on the process of learning and values discovery and creation of meaning through purposeful enquiry. Gerver highlights the positivity of mistakes as follows:

'To be successful you must respect failure and understand the power that not knowing can give you.' (p. 27)

While advocating this position Gerver acknowledges the system of schooling and analogises this to a high-stakes game show, where the risk of failure is not seen as an opportunity, but something to be avoided at all costs.

THE DAMAGE DONE

Assessment models

Extrapolating the effects of a disconnect between designing and making a little further, we can then predict what we expect from a creative activity and furthermore develop a hierarchy of values (independent of the learner/creator), that seamlessly translate into a marking scheme. This becomes problematic when you consider Sadler's (2009) perspective, that many uses of criterion-referenced assessment are sub-optimal, limiting both the teacher and student in the learning process. Furthermore, depending on students' perception of the relevance and purpose of the learning activity there are generally two outcomes, pragmatic and epistemic (Kirsh and Maglio, 1994). The pragmatist acts to address the given activity, while the students using epistemic actions augment their cognitive process, both potentially affecting the objectives of the educational experience. A disconnect between designing and making appears to define a standardised or convergent view of design activity. As a student you would be foolish not to try and predict 'what the assessor is looking for' and align your solution accordingly, resulting in a 'formulaic, routinised, and predictable' (Kimbell et al. 2004) reaction to design activity, framing its purpose and objectives. It is not clear how this supports a process of natural enquiry or our view of design education.

Pedagogy

Owen-Jackson (2000) highlights that from their inception, technological subjects were concerned with the didactic transposition of traditional knowledge and skills where 'Pupils were required only to learn the knowledge, not to understand it, and to copy and practise the making skills' (p. 5). Associated pedagogy demonstrated the procedural approach to develop specific skills and defined the required knowledge. Dakers (2005) presents the argument that;

> ' ... learning in this narrow model is linear and instrumental and to all intents and purposes, not meaningful learning at all. It is more concerned with the assimilation of the young into an already established value system which has more to do with control than it has to do with liberation.' (p. 113)

Presenting design as an activity independent of make and developing make skills independent of meaning will define a pedagogical practice that supports a 'safer' definition of what constitutes learning. Usher et al (1997) describes this as 'positivist epistemology of practice' where the dominant paradigm fails to resolve the dilemma of rigour versus relevance. Relevance must play a more significant constructivist role in learning.

CONCLUSIONS

The theoretical perspective that suggests 'designing' can be separated from 'making' really is a bad theory. Making is not solely the end of the design journey, but often the catalyst in refining design ideas. Making, experimenting, and modelling are an integral part of design thinking, and this relationship is critical to what we describe as good educational practice.

What is it we mean when we talk about creative activity? A general definition is the ability to transcend traditional ideas, relationship and practice and create new ideas, forms and methods that have value. From a particular perspective we sometimes make the assumption that we know definitively what is important for pupils to know. That we can predict the world, the problem, the contexts and situations that are and will be core to the lives of future generations. What if we are wrong? An alternative view is to consider the type of education a young person requires to sculpt and adapt this world for themselves and others. Can we create an environment that supports progressive thinking, enquiry, critique while developing disciplined knowledge and skills? Maybe the vision should be to support the development of transdisciplinary knowledge and skills in learning that is contextualised in continuous change and uncertainty.

This may sound ideological; but there are two points to note.
- This is not a new concept for a young person;
- and it is something that we have being achieving in Design and Technology education.

7. THE EDUCATIONAL PURPOSE OF DOING DESIGN PROJECTS
... Ken Baynes

It is important to be clear about the role of design projects in design education. Why should children and young people engage in designing and making as the main teaching and learning medium? The question is particularly sharp because most pupils will not become adult designers or makers. What the majority need is an understanding of designing and making as they affect their everyday lives and the big environmental and technological issues facing society.

Here are some of the arguments for the pedagogical value of designerly project work.

- Designerly thinking skills can only be developed by using them
- Making skills can only be developed through making
- Working on a realistic design project puts learning about theory into a relevant context
- Projects can be designed to allow for progression, development and differentiation
- Projects encourage a constructive interaction between the pupil and teacher in pursuit of a shared goal
- Projects can be designed to allow for individual and group work.
- Carefully chosen projects can allow the pupils to experience designing and making in a number of different fields or to pursue personal preferences and interests
- Carefully chosen projects can range from the highly speculative to the immediately useful and practical
- Projects encourage an assessment philosophy which really does value the 'journey' that the pupil has made. The pupil's own evaluation finds a logical place in the work.

Design and make projects also have a number of pitfalls. Two are particularly significant and are inter-related.

- There is a temptation to overvalue and hence to over-assess the finished product. Clearly, outcome needs to be seen as a window through which to view the learning experience rather than an end in itself. This perception has to be shared by pupils, teachers and assessors.
- There is often a mis-match between the pupil's imaginative vision and the pupil's ability to achieve it in reality. Since making skills are likely to always be emergent, the scope for disillusion is to some extent built into the situation. Good teaching can deal with this.

There exists a large body of experience relevant to good practice in organizing project-based work. This needs to be more widely known and to be given greater prominence in the professional training of teachers.

DESIGN EDUCATION PROJECTS

Eileen Adams

Education needs to create effective learners, for young people to learn how to learn, to be able to encounter new experiences, unfamiliar ideas and changing conditions confidently and creatively. Design education projects in schools help young people to develop capabilities that enable them to make sense of and operate effectively in a rapidly changing and increasingly complex world.

DESIGN

Design is about our material culture - artefacts, communications, places and systems. Design is influenced not only by economics, materials and technology, but also by historical precedent, cultural practices and fashion. Our environment is the result of myriad processes of thought and action, choices and decisions. These reflect values informing the ways we choose to live and to make our world. Design is about these values, choices and decisions. It is about relationships between people and place. It is about shaping and managing the environment. Making is central, but it is not only about making things: it is also about making sense, making meaning, and making things happen. Design is:

> '... essentially speculative and propositional. It is about the future. All its methods and procedures are directed towards deciding how places, products and images will be. In this respect, it is highly unusual in a curriculum dealing primarily with the past and what we already know. Design is not only knowing about the future it is about imagining it, shaping it and bringing it about. This needs to be emphasized and made real in learning.'   (Baynes, 1984).

Design is about dealing with change. Whether slow and imperceptible, or sudden and dramatic, maybe traumatic, change is the only certainty we have. Do we encourage young people to respond to new consumer products, to technology, or to environmental change with concern, self-confidence and good judgement? Or do they react with a vulnerable lack of awareness and understanding? What should our environment be like in the future? Young people are eager not only to respond to a changing world, but also want to help shape that world. We need to enable them to deal with the experience of change positively, creatively and responsibly, and see themselves as active players in the scene.

DESIGN EDUCATION: THE CHALLENGE

There is a need for education which questions how we choose to live, envisions better alternatives and addresses the issue of how we can work together to achieve improvement in environmental quality and a better quality of life. How best to support young people's learning in this complex, dynamic and multifaceted area, where the amount of information and knowledge that is available is more that we can assimilate, and the pace of development faster than we can deal with?

Design in schools has developed from technical education focused primarily on product design, locked into material technology and production processes. There needs to be a perceptual shift to create a broader view both of design and design education to embrace a more serious regard for our relationship with the environment, and our impact upon it. Educators need to consider *what* experience young people have of design, and *how* to extend their experience and deepen their understanding. Young people need to learn to understand how design shapes the physical and cultural milieu, to think about this critically, and to conceive of alternative possibilities for change and improvement. Design projects are an important strategy to engage young people with these challenges.

We need to be clearer and more sophisticated in our thinking about the notion of literacy. This is not just being able to read and write. It is about being able to participate in the world of ideas, the ideas that shape our society and our environment. It is important for young people to be able to participate not only in the discourse on design, but also to participate in the activity of design itself. Design education addresses this.

Design projects are as much about *how* young people learn as *what* they learn. Most importantly, we should question *why* they learn, and what they use their learning *for*. The starting points are how they *experience* their environment, how they are able to *make sense* of it, how they *respond* to it, what it *means* to them and to others, how it *impacts* upon them, and how they are able to *impact* upon it. How are they able to *deal with change* confidently, creatively and responsibly? How do they see themselves as *agents of change*?

DESIGN AND LEARNING

The word *design* acts as both noun and verb. It can imply both the content of what is learned and the activity of learning. Design education projects involve learning *about* design; learning *to* design; learning *through* design; learning *by* design; and learning *for* design.

We can learn *about* design if we just take a walk along the street, as long as we have developed the perceptual, analytical, interpretative and critical skills that enable us to make sense of our experience. We can learn *about* design if we have developed habits of attention and awareness, of intellectual enquiry and judgement. We can learn if we are open to experience and able to make connections with what we already know.

In learning to design, we might use the model of what professional designers do. This is generally interpreted as the processes of identifying a need or opportunity for change, research and investigation, ideas generation, experimentation, critique, developing and refining ideas, creating designs, models and prototypes, further testing, and finally production. Although this 'design loop' might serve as a useful framework for developing projects, it is not the only way to support learning, it does not necessarily develop designerly thinking, nor is it the way all designers work. Designers engage in the practice of design in many different ways, with multiple points of entry. We should keep in mind that we are engaging in educational practice. Adopting a model of professional design practice and applying it directly to learning activities in schools is not always appropriate. The most valuable outcome of projects with students is not what has been *designed*. It is what has been *learned*.

Learning *through* design is the educational model, and is the basis of projects in schools. It brings together learning *about* design and learning *to* design: design awareness and design activity.

> 'Three key questions worth asking pupils are: How did it come to be like that?; What value has it now?; and How should it be in the future?. The first emphasises the known, the second calls for critical analysis and judgement while the third encourages speculation and imagination and the application of knowledge and practical skills to human needs.' (Baynes, 2010).

The link between experience of design and designing is critical study, where young people develop skills to make informed judgements about aesthetic and design qualities, are helped to build a vocabulary and arguments to explain how they arrive at their judgements, and to give reasons for their opinions. The critic must explain responses, justify views, make comparisons, note influences, establish relationships and indicate a personal viewpoint.

In learning *through* design, emphasis is not so much on informational content as on learning strategies that enable students to understand, think and do things. Study involves a range of intellectual, practical and social skills. It relies on visual and spatial modes of thinking. It demands making connections between what is already known, relating this to new knowledge and gaining fresh insights. It requires students to see connections and juxtapositions. It involves judgement and decision-making. In addition to learning models of designer and critic, it brings into play those of researcher, scientist, artist and curator.

Learning *by* design is where the teacher creates a framework of experiences and activities for the students to learn. Teaching here is not merely instruction, or providing information, explanation or demonstration. It is creating situations and environments to support learning activities by encouraging certain attitudes, habits and methods of study, developing learning strategies and presenting an appropriate role model, the model of the good learner.

Learning *for* design might refer to training future professional designers. In schools, this is not the main aim, though hopefully some students may go into the design professions. More accurately, learning *for* design is about educating young people to be active as designers in their everyday lives, and to be able to participate as citizens in the process of adapting to changing circumstances creatively and responsibly.

LEARNING AND TEACHING

> 'Teaching and learning is the key arena for human development and change. It is here that the impact of curricula is felt, that teacher methods work well or not and that learners are motivated to participate and learn how to learn.'
>
> Unesco (2004).

What mindset prompts us to be excited about the world, about life, about ideas? How do we go about exploring these? And with what energy and drive do we do this? *Carefully chosen projects can allow the pupils to experience designing and making in a number of different fields or to pursue personal preferences and interests.* Design projects should be based on intellectual curiosity. How does something work? How can things be improved? Projects encourage certain ways of perceiving, knowing, responding to and interacting with the world. *Working on a realistic design project puts learning about theory into a relevant context.*

All learners have rich sources of prior knowledge, accumulated through a variety of experiences, which educators should draw out and nourish (Unesco, 2004). Design projects build on students' experience and knowledge: experience of everyday life, of people, of the environment, of material goods, of the media, of the Internet; and knowledge of how things look, feel, are made, and how they work – or fail to work. Projects offer stimulus and challenge for young people to interact with others, to shape their environment, to create feelings of pleasure and satisfaction, to create meaning in their lives. *Projects can be designed to allow for progression, development and differentiation*, so that the work relates to the young person's experience and interests, progressively opening up new intellectual challenges and requiring more depth of study as well as increasingly sophisticated levels of understanding.

Design education champions *experiential* learning, *investigative* learning, *authentic* learning. Just as we learn to walk, talk and read by trying to walk, talk and read, we learn design by trying to make and do things. We do not develop bike-riding skills while sitting at a desk. We get on a bike, try to pedal, fall off, get back on the bike and try again. We learn to ride a bike through the experience of handling and using a bike, experimentally and purposefully. We learn design through the experience of design and designing. *Designerly thinking skills can only be developed by using them. Making skills can only be developed through making.* Riding a bike does not only develop skills of balance and steering: it enables us to go somewhere.

Design education projects require approaches to learning and teaching that are based on the generation of new knowledge and the development of skills and capabilities that respond to the question *what would happen if?* The emphasis needs to be on helping young people learn how to learn: how to get to grips with new experiences, new ideas and new ways of thinking. This sits at odds with a system that still relies on transmission, absorption and regurgitation of information, didactic teaching methods, programmed learning and skills development.

THINKING

In design projects, students develop a range of thinking skills. They learn how to think about situations from different viewpoints, how to research and investigate, how to marshal and interpret information, and how to use a range of strategies to address problems. Not only do they use analytical skills, but they also learn to make connections, see relationships and synthesise disparate strands. Engaging in design projects develops young people's abilities to hypothesise and to visualise scenarios and possibilities as yet unknown. Imagination and fantasy are useful here, as are technical skills, to generate, develop and test out ideas before putting them into effect.

Intellectual, practical and technical skills are developed in all phases of the work. Design education involves both cognitive and affective modes of study: both objectivity and subjectivity are valued. Skills of empathy are evident in pupils' responses to environments, products and communications, and in their understanding of people's needs. Intuition has a part to play: designing requires insights and creative leaps to make connections and establish relationships. Problem identification and problem solving require young people to make connections, develop insights, make informed guesses and follow up hunches, which require empathy and intuition.

THINKING TOOLS

In most subjects, it is primarily words and numbers that make thinking possible. However, in design projects, visual and spatial literacy come into play. Students use images and three-dimensional media to develop visual and spatial skills - drawings, maps, plans, diagrams, blueprints, patterns, photomontage, photographs, digital images, sketch models and prototypes.

Drawing has particular significance in design projects: different kinds of drawing prompt different kinds of thinking. Drawing as *perception* is that which assists the ordering of sensations, feelings, ideas and thoughts. Here, drawing might enable students to explore and develop observation and interpretative skills to investigate and understand the world. Drawing as *invention* is that which assists the creative manipulation and development of thought. Ideas are at an embryonic stage, unformed or only partly formed at the beginning of the process of drawing. Ideas take shape when the drawer experiences reflexive oscillation between impulse, ideas and mark, receiving feedback from the marks appearing on the page, which prompt further thought and mark-making. Usually the drawing is one of a series, where ideas are explored, repeated, refined, practised, worked over, discarded, combined, where alternatives are sought and alternative possibilities explored. Drawing as *communication* is that which assists the process of making ideas, thoughts and feelings available to others. Here, the intention is to communicate sensations, feelings or ideas to someone else. It is likely that certain codes or conventions will be used so that the viewer will be helped to understand what is being communicated. Drawing as *action* is that which assists in the making and implementation of plans. Here the intention is to anticipate, explain, describe an activity, a process or sequence of events.

Design projects create opportunities for students to generate, appropriate and manipulate images to develop thinking. Working with their own photographs, or those of others, most likely downloaded from the Internet, editing and manipulating them, students are able to shape and communicate ideas. Annotated photographs, photomontage and photomaps link images with words and numbers. Computer technology enables students to test out different configurations very quickly, and also opens up opportunities for time-based work, evident in animation, film and computer-aided environmental design.

Although form, space and volume can be simulated on a computer screen, working directly in three dimensions is extremely valuable. Sketch models that students construct and handle are useful to explore ideas at an early stage, and experimentation with materials often throws up new forms and relationships. Conceptual models help to develop ideas, especially in collaborative work, when elements can be changed easily and different versions compared. Prototypes allow rigorous testing. Presentational models communicate ideas to others who have not been involved in the design process.

Words allow students to question, comment, explain, argue, debate, justify - all necessary for critical study. Skills of listening and speaking are necessary at all stages, in dialogue between student and teacher; during research and investigations: in analysis and interpretation of research material, in group work and design activity, and in presentations and critique. It is also important for students to be able to articulate what they have learned and to explain their learning process.

ATTITUDES, VALUES, DISPOSITIONS AND CAPABILITIES

Skills are developed through experience and practice. They disappear unless they are used. But design education is not merely learning a skill set. It is about developing a complex set of dispositions and capabilities that result in designerly thinking. This is a combination of qualities and attitudes, a frame of mind that involves students being open to new experience, willing to experiment and prepared to take risks. They learn to be able to deal with ambiguity and complexity, cope with disappointment and treat the experience of frustration and failure positively.

Design is often linked with creativity. Ken Robinson describes creativity as *imaginative activity fashioned so as to produce outcomes that are both original and of value*, and identifies four characteristics of creative processes:

- *They always involve thinking or behaving imaginatively.*

- *This imaginative activity is purposeful, directed to achieving an objective.*

- *These processes must generate something original.*

- *The outcome must be of value in relation to the objective* (Robinson, 1999).

Creative activity does not exist in a vacuum. It is generally in response to a stimulus, a challenge or a disturbance, when we need to sort something out, work something out or resolve a problem. Young people learn best when they feel that their work is purposeful. Creativity is evident not just in our response to what exists, but to conceive of *things as yet unseen* (Read, 1946). Design projects encourage young people to use their powers of imagination and invention to create a bridge between what is seen and felt to that which is thought, imagined and realised. Dispositions that support creativity include the ability to wonder, to question, to be playful, to experiment, to take risks, to value difference, to collaborate with others and to explore different points of view.

For something to be creative, we might expect it to be original, unique, innovative or novel. For young people's work, it is enough if it is new for them. Learning should result in their being able to think something they could not think beforehand, understand something that was not clear to them, or do something they could not do previously. Young people's originality should not be compared with that of adult professionals. Design education projects nurture young people's urge to make things, to do things, to change things through re-working their own experience and recycling the ideas of others to shape their thinking and actions. Here, strategies such as appropriation, adaptation and transformation are useful.

LEARNER

Our education system currently emphasises system rather than education. Education bureaucrats offer *packages* and *service delivery*, models based on consumerism, which take away young people's responsibility to develop as active and independent learners. As parents and teachers do more of their thinking for them, organising their time and their activities, controlling access to educational, environmental and social experience, solving problems and making decisions, young people's capacity to learn is increasingly limited. We must nurture their capabilities as independent learners, and pay attention to ways they are helped *how* to learn and the manner in which they are encouraged to love learning.

In design projects, a framework for study is negotiated, and students contribute ideas and ways of working. Each is encouraged to bring experience, ideas and insights to the work. Developing opportunities for independent learning through design education increases opportunities to develop imaginative and creative thinking. Although the Internet provides a wonderful research tool, it is increasingly shaping young people's view of the world, and limiting their opportunities to acquire practical and social skills from direct experience. Instead of being viewers and voyeurs, they should learn to be thinkers, makers and doers.

Projects can be designed to allow for both individual and group work. Learning through design involves both personal initiative and collaborative working. Skills of cooperation and taking shared responsibility are important for later life. So too are communication skills of presentation, argument and persuasion, all of which are developed through group work in design projects. There is a need to vary the roles within groups from time to time, so that each student has experience of leading an activity, and those who tend to dominate or withdraw can be supported to contribute usefully in a variety of ways. Social and interpersonal skills are required in team-working and shared decision-making.

TEACHER

Design education projects cut across the traditional boundaries of subjects and address wider curriculum concerns, such as citizenship and education for sustainability. Individual subject teachers cannot manage design education alone: it requires contributions from different disciplines. However, teachers working separately, or even in parallel, does not always result in young people developing a coherent view of design, or result in their being able to apply their knowledge to their everyday lives. Design education requires not only multi-disciplinary approaches, but also interdisciplinary strategies, to help young people make connections and exploit synergies. Design projects provide opportunities for staff and students to work together outside the confines of the subject-based curriculum. They can prompt changes in working relationships within the school as well as with agencies outside the school. They can redefine roles and relationships between learners and teachers.

The challenge is to create the environment and conditions where learning can develop and flourish through good teaching. Most importantly, the educator's role is to model how to learn, and to help students to make use of the results of their learning. Teachers bring into play knowledge of how young people learn and strategies for supporting learning. The teacher must motivate and inspire; provide a range of stimulus; clarify expectations, establish parameters and frameworks for learning; structure and shape learning experiences; provide guidance, suggest possible directions; explain approaches and demonstrate techniques; question, challenge and disturb.

Projects encourage a constructive interaction between the pupil and teacher in pursuit of a shared goal. Projects introduce students to learning experiences and working relationships different from other areas of the curriculum. A major difference is that the teacher does not know the outcome before the students embark on the project. In opposition to current orthodoxy, in design, learning outcomes must not be predetermined. The point of engaging in a design education project is to learn something new, to generate ideas, understandings and meanings, not to absorb and regurgitate what is already known. If the result is predetermined, there is no point in doing the project. The teacher provides feedback, values students' efforts and helps them evaluate their work to acknowledge what has been learned.

LEARNING OUTCOMES

Learning outcomes are what students are able to understand, think and be capable of doing as a result of their learning experience. These are evident in students' perceptions, thoughts, attitudes and actions. Drawings, diagrams, mock-ups and prototypes are not the outcomes: they are merely some of the evidence of the students' learning journey. *Projects encourage an assessment philosophy which really does value the journey that the pupil has made. The pupil's own evaluation finds a logical place in the work.*

In summary, design education projects nurture a wide range of transferable, intellectual and practical skills through purposeful application and practice in appropriate contexts. The range is enormous, enabling young people to develop abilities to: analyse, annotate, appreciate, argue, articulate, assimilate, build, categorise, change, choose, classify, codify, compare, conceive, connect, construct, contrast, control, cooperate, demonstrate, differentiate, depict, describe, discriminate, discover, draft, dream, engage, enjoy, examine, experience, experiment, explain, enquire, explore, express, extrapolate, fantasise, feel, focus, formalise, formulate, generate ideas, grasp ideas, hypothesise, identify, illustrate, imagine, interpret, invent, investigate, judge, know, label, locate, look, make, measure, manipulate, match, modify, narrate, observe, order organise, participate, perceive, persist, persuade, play, question, reason, recall, recognise, reflect, relate, remember, respond, see, select, sequence, shape, show, sort, structure, symbolise, synthesise, transform, try, understand, validate, visualise, watch, wish and wonder.

As a result of design projects, we should look for evidence of young people being effective learners in a range of contexts and enable them to apply the results of their learning in a variety of settings, beyond the boundaries of the classroom, and through non-formal and lifelong learning activities. We should expect to see evidence of young people using and enriching their learning through engagement with their local community, through participation in environmental issues and environmental action, through sharing ideas on the Web, through being part of the cultural milieu outside the school. Literacy is not about being able to read and write; it is about shaping the ideas that shape our society. Design education is about developing our capacity to learn, enabling us to understand, to think and to do things. We need to invigorate design education in schools with new purposes and new directions. Design education projects offer useful strategies.

FINAL WORD

Ken Baynes

There appears to be wide agreement amongst our contributors as to the nature of design education.

Design education can be regarded as a third focus for the curriculum. It is clearly orientated towards the future. It is practical and deals with some of the most important issues facing humanity. But it is also relevant at a personal level and provides a range of very valuable life skills.

The contributors agree that all humans possess potential design ability and can understand design. However, these potentials will remain unrealized if they are not deliberately fostered by education. It is agreed that design education should both encourage and develop the skills of those who will later join the design professions and also of the population at large. They will benefit in their own day-to-day lives but also be able to make a more informed contribution to some of the key issues now challenging democracies.

Education claims to be 'relevant' and nearly everyone agrees that relevance is a desirable thing. However, the curriculum looks less and less relevant to the nature of the 21st century. Making design education a factor in every child's school experience would go a long way to providing relevance.

Design clearly crosses subject boundaries. Should it therefore be a new embracing area in the curriculum or should it be a dimension of many subjects ? The reality is that design IS a dimension of many subjects. Our contributors make this point clear. However, design education has suffered from appearing in the titles of two National Curriculum subject areas: Art and Design and Design and Technology. There is a danger in being everyone's baby and yet no-one's favourite child. The model of language might be helpful. Linguistic expression is important in nearly every school subject, yet the English teacher has the responsibility for developing and promoting the subject. To thrive, design education needs a firm base but also recognition in the wider curriculum.

Assessment methods in design need to reflect the nature of designing. Since projects are an essential learning medium in design, the assessment of projects should be the fundamental methodology in design. Much experience in this field exists and now needs to be 're-discovered'.

Design is a very visual subject. Although designers are concerned with their impact on all the human senses, vision – in the form of modelling 'seeing in the mind's eye' – is essential to the development and communication of design ideas. Visual qualities are also central to the way non-designers understand and interact with the designed world. 'Graphicacy' or visual education is therefore very important for design education, a concern it must pursue in close cooperation with, for example, art, geography, mathematics and other subjects which use visual imagery, symbols and codes.

REFERENCES

DESIGN EDUCATION RESEARCH

Ólafsson B and Thorsteinsson G (2009) 'Design and craft education in Iceland, pedagogical background and development: a literature review', *Design and technology Education: an international journal,* 14(3), pp 10-24
http://ojs.lboro.ac.uk/ojs/index.php/DATE/article/view/246

Norman E W L , Mitchell A, Zanker N P and Patterson, A 'Developing the Research Infrastructure for design and technology education in England (and beyond)', *PATT2009,* M J de Vries(ed), September 2009, TUDelft University
http://www.iteaconnect.org/Conference/PATT/PATT22/Norman.pdf

Norman E (2011) 'The nature of effective research contributions in design education'. In Bohemia, E, Borja de Mozota, B, Collina, L (eds) *Researching Design Education: Ist International Symposium for Design Education Researchers*, Paris, pp 52-68
http://collab.northumbria.ac.uk/2011paris/?page_id=2

van den Akker J, Gravemeijer K, McKenney S and Nieveen N (2006) (eds), *Educational Design Research*, London and New York: Routledge

THE EMPTY SPACE

The 2010 John Eggleston Memorial Lecture was given by Ken Baynes at the *D&T - Ideas Worth Sharing: The Design and Technology Association Education & International Research Conference*. The lecture was entitled: 'Models of Change: The future of design education' and the published version can be freely downloaded from:
http://ojs.lboro.ac.uk/ojs/index.php/DATE/article/view/1532

Since a large part of the lecture was a reflection on many years of direct experience, it does not lend itself to conventional referencing. However, here are some avenues for further reading and research.

- *Cognitive modelling and design*
  Much of the background can be found in the Loughborough University Orange Series *Models of Change* based on the series of seminars given by Ken Baynes during 2009/10. These are available online at:
  https://dspace.lboro.ac.uk/dspace-jspui/handle/2134/1686

- *Bruce Archer and design education in the 1970s*
  See the D&TA/DERG publication:
  Bruce Archer, Ken Baynes and Phil Roberts, *A Framwork for Design and Design Education: a reader containing key papers from the 1970s and 80s* (2005). This is available from the Design and Technology Association or online at:
  http://www.data.org.uk/generaldocs/dater/Framework%20for%20Design.pdf

- *For more on neuroscience:*
  Pinker S (1998), *How the Mind Works*, London, Allen Lane: the Penguin Press. Originally published by W W Norton, 1997.

  Zecki S (1999) *Inner Vision, an exploration of art and the brain*, Oxford: Oxford University Press

SEVEN KEY THEMES

Theme 1 The Aims of Design Education

Archer B (nd, but early 1970s), *Time for a revolution in art and design education,* London: Royal College of Art

Archer B (1975) 'A closer look at the relations between the broad concept of design in general education and its component parts', Midland Art Advisors Conference Paper, 6 May, London: Royal College of Art

Roberts P H, Archer B and Baynes K (1992) *Modelling: The Language of Designing,* Design: Occasional Paper No1, Department of Design & Technology, Loughborough University 1992, downloadable from: https://dspace.lboro.ac.uk/2134/1689

Roberts P H (1982) , 'Learning to mean', *Design Studies,* 3(4), October, pp 205-211

Theme 2 The Significance of Practical Education

Baynes B (2013), *Design: Models of Change.* Shepshed: Loughborough Design Press

Brochocka K and Baynes K (2013), unpublished report for The Harley Gallery, Welbeck, Nottinghamshire

Burke P (1972), *Traditions and Innovation in Renaissance Italy,* London: B T Batsford Ltd, (Original title *Culture and Society in Renaissance Italy,* changed for the Fontana Edition, 1974)

Chapman R, (1993)*The Complete Guitarist,* London: Dorling Kindersley

Daley J (1982), ' Design creativity and the understanding of objects' *Design Studies,* 3(3) pp 133-137. (Reprinted in 1984, *Developments in Design Methodology,* N Cross (ed), New York: John Wiley)

Denyer R (1982), *The Guitar Handbook,* London: Dorling Kindersley

Fletcher N H and Rossing T D (1998), *The Physics of Musical instruments (Second Edition),* New York: Springer-Verlag

Jahnel F(1981), *Manual of Guitar Technology: the History and Technology of Plucked String Instruments (First English Edition),* Westport: The Bold Strummer Ltd

Glancey J (2012), *Giants of Steam.* London: Atlantic Books

Huber J (1994), *The Development of the Modern Guitar,* (English Edition), London: Kahn & Avril

Pedgely O F (1999) 'Industrial Designers' Attention to Materials and Manufacturing Processes: Analyses at Macroscopic and Microscopic Levels,' *Ph.D. thesis,* Department of Design and Technology, Loughborough University

Pedgley O F, Norman E and Armstrong R (2009), 'Materials-Inspired Innovation for Acoustic Guitar Design,' *METU Journal of the Faculty of Architecture,* 26(1) , pp 157-175

Pedgley O F and Norman E (2012) 'Materials Innovation in Acoustic Guitars: Challenging the Tonal Superiority of Wood', *Leonardo Music Journal*, 22, pp 17–24

Shahar S (1990), *Childhood in the Middle Ages*. London: Routledge

Richardson B (1994*)*, 'The acoustical development of the guitar', *Journal of The Catgut Acoustical Society,* 2(5), pp 1-10

Wheeler T (1981), *The Guitar Book,* Macdonald Futura Publishers

Theme 3 Encouraging the Imagination

Ashiabi G S (2007), 'Play in the preschool classroom: Its socioemotional significance and the teacher's role in play', *Early Childhood Education Journal*, 35, pp 199-207

Bartel M (2010), *Some Possible Reasons for the Drop in Divergent Thinking*
www.bartlart.com/arted/drop-in-divergent-thinking.html

Bartel M (2009), *The Secrets of Generating Art Ideas*
www.bartelart.com/arted/ideas.html

Boden M (2001), 'Creativity and knowledge'. In A Craft, B. Jeffrey & M Leibling (eds), *Creativity in Education*. London: Continuum, pp 95-102

Callahan R M (1992), *Imagining imagination: A phenomenological study of children's drawings of imagination: a dissertation*
http://archive.org/details/imaginingimagina00robe

Craft A (2000), *Creativity across the primary curriculum*, London: Routledge

Craft A (2002), *Creativity and Early Years Education*, London: Continuum

Emmenegger P (2012), 'Nurturing the playful mind', *Natural Child Magazine.*
www.naturalchildmagazine.com/0804/Nuturing_the_Playful_Mind.htm

Gardner H (2007), *The Five Minds of the Future*. Watertown, MA: Harvard Business Press

Haskvitz A (2006), *Tapping into your child's imagination: Ten steps.* (Reach every child: Resources for teachers and students)
www.reacheverychild.com/feature/imagination.html

Jenkins J M & Astington J W (2000), 'Theory of mind and social behaviour: Casual models tested in a longitudinal study', *Merrill-Palmer Quarterly*, 46, pp 203-220
http://jenkinslab.files.wordpress.com/2009/08/article_csc_jenkinsastington2000.pdf

Law E L-C. (2007), 'Technology-enhanced creativity'. In A-G Tan (ed) *Creativity: A Handbook for Teachers,* Singapore: World Scientific Publishing pp 363-383

National Advisory Committee on Creativity and Cultural Education (NACCCE) (1999), *All Our Futures: Creativity, Culture and Education,* London, DfEE

Neilson M (2012), 'Imitation, pretend play, and childhood: Essential elements in the evolution of human culture?', *Journal of Comparative Psychology*, 126, pp170-181

Norman R. (2000), 'Cultivating imagination in adult education', *Proceedings of 41ˢᵗ Annual Adult Education Research.* www.adulterc.org/Proceedings/2000/normanr-final.PDF

Ochse R (1990), *Before the Gates of Excellence: The Determinants of Creative Genius*, Cambridge: Cambridge University Press

Pelaprat E & Cole M (2011), ''Minding the Gap': Imagination, creativity and human cognition', *Integrative Psychological and Behavioural Science*, 45, pp 397-418 http://lchc.ucsd.edu/mca/Paper/ETMCimagination.pdf

Russ S W (2003), 'Play and creativity: developmental issues', *Scandinavian Journal of Educational Research*, 47(3), pp 291-303 www.tandfonline.com/doi/abs/10.1080/00313830308594

Singer D G & Singer J L (2005). *Imagination and play in the electronic age,* Cambridge, MA: Harvard University Press

Singer J L & Lythcott M A (2004), 'Fostering school achievement and creativity through sociodramatic play in the classroom'. In E. F. Zigler, D. G. Singer & S. J. Bishop-Joseph (eds) *Children's play: The roots of reading,* Washington DC: Zero to Three Press, pp 77-93

Taylor M, Carlson S M, & Shawber A B (2009), 'Children's imaginary companions: What it is like to have an invisible friend?'. In K. Markman, W. Klein, & J. Suhr (eds) *The handbook of imagination and mental stimulation*, New York: Psychology Press, pp 211-224

Taylor M, Carlson S M, Maring B L, Gerow L, & Charley C (2004), 'The characteristics and correlates of high fantasy in school-aged children: imaginary companions, impersonation and social understanding', *Developmental Psychology,* 40, pp1173-1187

Viereck, 'What life means to Einstein', *Saturday Evening Post*, Oct.26 1929 www.saturdayeveningpost.com/wp-content/uploads/satevepost/what_life_means_to_einstein.pdf

Vygotsky L S (2004), 'Imagination and creativity in childhood' (English translation M. E. Sharpe), *Journal of Russian and East European Psychology* 42(1), pp 7-97

Wang S (2009), *The Power of Magical Thinking*, The Wall Street Journal December 22ⁿᵈ 2009 http://online.wsj.com/article/SB10001424052748703344704574610002061841322.html

Warren Z (2011), 'Who values children's imagination? The effect of religious orthodoxy on human values in 16 western countries', www.academia.edu/525664/Who_values_childrens_imagination_The_effect_of_religious_orthodoxy_on_human_values_in_16_Judeo-Christian_countries

Theme 4 The Cognitive Value of Aesthetic Awareness

Banham R *(1960),* *Theory and Design in the First Machine Age*, London: The Architectural Press

Beh, C-S and Norman, E (2010) 'Visual communication of technology for designing and its links to creativity and Innovation'. In Spendlove D and Stables K (eds) *D&T – Ideas Worth Sharing: The Design and Technology Association Education and International Conference*, Wellesbourne: The Design and Technology Association, pp 13-28

Baynes K and Pugh F (1981), *The Art of the Engineer*. Guildford:The Lutterworth Press

Campaign for Drawing by Eileen Adams, which are available at:
www.drawingpower.org.uk

Danos X, Norman E, Storer I and Robson J (2010), 'Identifying Continuity and Progression in the Development of Graphicacy'. In Spendlove D and Stables K (eds) *D&T – Ideas Worth Sharing: The Design and Technology Association Education and International Conference*, Wellesbourne: The Design and Technology Association, pp 33-52

Dissanayake E (1995), *Home Aestheticus: Where art comes from and why*. Seattle: University of Washington Press. (First published by The Free Press, 1992)

McKay A (1978), *Vitruvius Architect and Engineer*. Bristol: Bristol Classical Press, 1985. (Originally published Macmillan Education Ltd)

Pinker S (1998), *How the Mind Works*, London, Allen Lane: the Penguin Press. Originally published by W W Norton, 1997

Pye D (1964), *The Nature of Design*, London: Studio Vista

Read H (1943), *Education through Art*, London: Faber and Faber

Wilson E O (2012), *The Social Conquest of Earth*, New York: Liveright Publishing Corporation

Zeki S (1999), *Inner Vision: an exploration of art and the brain*. Oxford: Oxford University Press

Theme 5 The Value of Learning through Making

Barnes J (2007) *Cross-curricular Learning 3-14;* London: Paul Chapman Publishing

Buchanan R (1995), 'Wicked problems in design thinking'. In Margolin V & Buchanan R (eds.) *The Idea of Design*, Massachusetts: MIT

Csikszentmihalyi M.(1988), *Optimal Experience: Psychological Studies of Flow in Consciousness*, Cambridge, UK: Cambridge University

Davies D, Howe A, & Ritchie R (2001) *Primary Design & Technology for the Future: Creativity, Culture & Citizenship*, David Fulton Publishers

DfEE/QCA (1990), *National Curriculum for Design and Technology*, London: Department for Education and Employment/Qualifications and Curriculum Authority

DfEE/QCA (1993), *National Curriculum for Design and Technology,* London: Department for Education and Employment/Qualifications and Curriculum Authority

DfEE/QCA (1999), *The National Curriculum Key Stages 1 & 2*, London: Department for Education and Employment and Qualifications and Curriculum Authority

Harrison A(1978), *Making & Thinking*, London:The Harvester Press

Hope G (2002), *Drawing as a Tool for Thought* (unpublished Ph.D. thesis), University of London

Hope G (2005), 'The types of drawings that young children produce in response to design tasks', *Design and Technology Education: an international journal*, 10(1), Wellesbourne: The Design and Technology Association, pp 45-53

Hope G (2006), *Teaching Design and Technology in Key Stages 1 and 2*, Exeter: Learning Matters

Hope G, Yusef Z M and Vengrasalam R (2011), 'Technology in Malaysian primary schools'. In Benson, C. and Lunt, J. (eds.) *International Handbook of Primary Technology Education: Reviewing the Past Twenty Years*, Rottendam: Sense Publishers

Middleton H (2000), 'Design and Technology: What is the problem?' In Kimbell R (ed) *Design and Technology International Millennium Conference 2000*, Wellesbourne: The Design and Technology Association, pp116-120

Parkinson E F (2012), (unpublished Ph.D. thesis), Canterbury Christ Church University

Rittel H & Webber M M (1973), 'Wicked problems' (extracts from 'Dilemmas in a general theory of planning', *Policy Sciences*, 4). In Cross N, Elliott D & Roy R (eds) *Man-Made Futures* (1976), Milton Keynes: Open University Press, pp 272-280

Roberts P H (1992), 'Of models, modelling & design: an applied philosphical enquiry'. In Roberts P H, Archer B and Baynes K (eds) *Modelling: The Language of Designing*, Design: Occasional Paper No1, Department of Design & Technology, Loughborough University 1992, downloadable from: https://dspace.lboro.ac.uk/2134/1689

Stables K, Rogers M, Kelly C, and Fokias F (2001), *Enriching Literacy through Design and Technology Evaluation Project*, London: Goldsmith College; University of London

Theme 6 The Creative Relationships between Designing and Making

Canty D (2012), *The Impact of Holistic Assessment using Adaptive Comparative Judgement on Student Learning*, PhD Thesis, University of Limerick, Limerick Ireland

Claxton, G (2008), *What's the point of school? Rediscovering the Hearth of Education*, Oxford, England: Oneworld Publications

Conklin J (2006) 'Wicked problems & social complexity', (Chapter 1 of *Dialogue Mapping: Building Shared Understanding of Wicked Problems*, Chichester, West Sussex: Wiley) downloadable from:
http://www.cognexus.org/wpf/wickedproblems.pdfi

Dakers J (2005), 'The hegemonic behaviorist cycle', *International Journal of Technology and Design Education*, 15, pp 111-126

Dow W (2006), 'The need to change pedagogies in science and technology subjects: a European perspective', *International Journal of Technology and Design Education*, 16, pp 307-321

Evans M, Pei E and Campbell R I (2010), *ID cards: a taxonomy of design representations to support communication and understanding during new product development*, downloadable from:
http://www.lboro.ac.uk/media/wwwlboroacuk/content/lds/downloads/research/researchgroups/designpractice/id-cards.pdf

Fish J, Scrivener S (1990), *Amplifying the Mind's Eye: Sketching and Visual Cognition*. Leonardo, 23, pp 117-126

Gerver R, (2010) *Creating Tomorrows Schools Today Education- Our Children – Their Future* London: Continuum International Publishing Group

Kim J, Bouchard C, Omhover J F, Aoussat A, Moscardini L, Chevalier A, Tijus C, & Buron F (2009), 'A Study on Designer's Mental Process of Information Categorization in the Early Stages of Design', *Generation of New Image-based and User-centered Solutions for Design*, Paris, download from:
http://www.mangold-international.com/fileadmin/Media/References/Publications/Downloads/Designers_Mental_Process_IASDR09.pdf

Kimbell R (2004), 'Ideas and Ideation', *The Journal of Design and Technology Education*, 9(3), pp 136-137

Kimbell R, Stables K, Wheeler T, Miller S, Bane J, & Wright R (2004). *Assessing Design Innovation,* London: Department of Education and Skills

Kirsh D and Maglio P (1994), 'On distinguishing epistemic from pragmatic action', *Cognitive Science*, 18, pp 513-549

Kolb, D (1984) *Experiential Learning as the Science of Learning and Development*, Englewood Cliffs, NJ: Prentice Hall

Lane D (2011), *Developing Sketching Expertise within Technology Education*, PhD Thesis, University of Limerick, Limerick Ireland

Lewin K (1952), *Field Theory in Social Science: Selected theoretical papers by Kurt Lewin*, London, UK: Tavistock

Owen-Jackson G (2000), 'Design and technology in the school curriculum'. In Owen-Jackson G (Ed.), *Learning to Teach Design and Technology in the Secondary School,* London: Routledge Falmer, pp 1–9

Pei E (2009), *Building a Common Language of Design Representations for Industrial Designers & Engineering Designers*, PhD Thesis, Loughborough University, downloadable from:
http://hdl.handle.net/2134/5432

Sadler D R (2009), 'Transforming Holistic Assessment and Grading into a Vehicle for Complex Learning'. In Joughin G (ed.) *Assessment, Learning and Judgement in Higher Education*, Springer Science+Business Media, pp 45 - 63

Usher R, Bryant I and Johnston R (1997), *Adult Education and the Postmodern Challenge*, London: Routledge

Welch M (1997) 'Year 7 students use of three-dimensional modelling while designing and making', *IDATER 1997 Conference*, Loughborough: Loughborough University, downloadable from http://hdl.handle.net/2134/1469

Welch M and Lim H S (1999) 'Teaching sketching and its effect on the solutions produced by novice designers', *IDATER 1999 Conference*, Loughborough: Loughborough University downloadable from http://hdl.handle.net/2134/1442

Theme 7 The Educational Purpose of Doing Design Projects

Baynes K (1984), paper presented at the National Society for Art Education Conference, Bath

Baynes K, (2010), 'Models of Change: the future of design education', *Design and Technology Education: An International Journal,* 15(3), pp 10-17
http://ojs.lboro.ac.uk/ojs/index.php/DATE/article/view/1532/1486

Read H, (1946), *The Grass Roots of Art: Lectures on the Social Aspects of Art in an Industrial Age*, London: Faber and Faber.

Robinson K (1999), *All Our Futures: Creativity, Culture and Education* in National Advisory Committee on Creative and Cultural Education, , London: Department for Education and Employment

Unesco (2004), *Education for All: The Quality Imperative*, Paris

AUTHOR PROFILES

Eileen Adams

Eileen Adams is a freelance consultant whose work links art, design, environment and education. In her career over 40 years, she has worked as a teacher, teacher educator, researcher, consultant, examiner, evaluator and writer. In the 1970s research interests included themes such as experiential learning, inter-professional collaboration in education and young people's participation in environmental change. In the 1980s, she investigated the school as a learning environment. In the 1990s, public art featured. Since 2001, Eileen's work has focused on learning through drawing. She shares the results of her work through publications, conference papers and courses in the UK and internationally.

Stephanie Atkinson

Stephanie Atkinson is a Professor of Design and Technology Education at the University of Sunderland. She has undergraduate qualifications as a Product and Furniture Designer from Northumbria University and a PhD from Newcastle-upon-Tyne University. Stephanie has held senior appointments in design and technology at all levels: in schools as Head of 3D Studies, as lecturer at Loughborough University and as Principal Lecturer, Reader and now Professor at University of Sunderland. Her early research for her PhD focused on the de-motivation of pupils in schools, but more recently she has been investigating the design activity of students training to become teachers in terms of designing styles and the relationship between such factors as learning styles, creativity, gender and computer aided learning, with many international publications to her name. She is a member of three international journal's editorial boards, examines PhDs internationally, is an external examiner for several universities and is the external advisor for Design and Technology for the International Baccalaureate Organisation and Edexcel. In 2010 the Design and Technology Association presented her with an award for 'Outstanding Contribution to Design and Technology Education' and in 2011 she was awarded an MBE in the Queen's Birthday Honours for services to Higher Education.

Ken Baynes

Ken Baynes' initial education was as a stained glass designer at a rural art school in Devon and the Royal College of Art in London. However, he has spent his professional career working as a designer, cultural historian and advocate of design education. At the centre of his work, have been two main themes: the use of exhibitions as a medium for education and entertainment and the attempt to develop better strategies for teaching art and design. He was Head of the Design Education Unit at the Royal College of Art and a Visiting Professor at the Loughborough Design School. Working with the Welsh Arts Council he developed a series of pioneering exhibitions that explored the relationship between art and society. With his wife Krysia he has specialized in exhibitions that appeal to children and family groups and which emphasize making and aesthetic awareness. They have been shown in London, Scandinavia, Edinburgh, Glasgow and the United States. He worked with Malachite to research and present two television series on design for Channel 4. His books include *About Design*, *Art in Society* and (with Francis Pugh) *The Art of the Engineer*.

Krysia Brochocka

Krysia Brochocka is an independent educational and design consultant. Her background is in primary education, ceramics and design education. She has taught at all school levels, teacher training and degree courses in ceramics and design education. For the past twenty years, Krysia has worked with Ken Baynes in conceptualizing and organizing exhibitions in museums and art galleries. During this time she was also involved in developing educational books and magazines for art, design and food. Throughout her career she has continued to do research, particularly into aesthetic awareness and design education. She has been commissioned by the Design Council, Scottish Natural Heritage, Crafts Council and various local authorities. She was a member of the Assessment of Performance Unit and the Design and Technology National Curriculum Working Group.

Christopher Frayling

Professor Sir Christopher Frayling was until recently Rector of the Royal College of Art and Chair of Arts Council England. He was also Chair of the Design Council, of the Crafts Study Centre and of the Royal Mint Design Advisory Committee. An historian, a critic, a curator and an award-winning broadcaster on network radio and television, he has written eighteen books on art, design and popular culture - the most recent being 'Ken Adam -The Art of Production Design' (Faber) and "On Craftsmanship - towards a new Bauhaus' (Oberon). His most recent exhibition, which he co-curated, was the record-breaking 'Hollywood Costume' at the V&A. He has been a member of the Crafts Council, of the Arts and Humanities Research Council (for which he campaigned), and was the longest-serving Trustee of the Victoria and Albert Museum. In 2000, he was knighted for "services to art and design education". Christopher is currently Professor Emeritus of Cultural History at the RCA, a Fellow of Churchill College Cambridge, a Commissioner for the Great Exhibition of 1851, a Visiting Professor at the University of Lancaster and a member of the board of the Design Museum. He has just completed a book on cultural anxieties in the West about China over the last two hundred years.

Gill Hope

Since 2002, Dr Gill Hope has been a Senior Lecturer in design and technology education at Canterbury Christ Church University, Kent. She has written extensively about design and technology in the Primary school, through research papers and journal articles as well as being the author of 3 books on the subject. Her most recent book, *Thinking and Learning through Drawing*, developed from her PhD inquiry into young children using drawing for designing. She travels extensively, both for pleasure and to attend international conferences, and her knowledge of German, French and Spanish enables her to gain insights into viewpoints from other countries across the world. From 2005-2008 she was part of a team of experts consulted by the Malaysian government to update initial teacher education for Primary schools.

Eddie Norman

Eddie Norman is Emeritus Professor of Design Education at Loughborough Design School (LDS), UK. His research concerns the relationship of technologies and designing in relation to general and higher education, and associated pedagogical issues. He was leader of the Design Education Research Group, published widely and supervised 7 PhD students. He contributed to teaching at LDS on undergraduate and masters design programmes. He has been an External Examiner for undergraduate and masters programmes and PhD research submissions (eg Bath Spa, Brunel, Goldsmiths, NIE Singapore and the University of Limerick). He remains Editor of *Design and Technology Education: an international journal* and has recently founded the specialist publisher Loughborough Design Press Ltd with Ken Baynes. Prior to joining LDS he had careers both in secondary education and as a professional engineer.

Phil Roberts

Phil Roberts is Emeritus Professor, Loughborough University. Professional experience includes appointments as Head of Design Faculty; Deputy Headteacher; Tutor & Research Supervisor, Department of Design Research & Design Education Unit, Royal College of Art; LEA Inspector (Art & Design); HM Inspectorate (Art & Design); sometime General Secretary, & Chair, National Association for Design Education (NADE); sometime Hon Secretary, Confederation of Art & Design Associations (CADA). Formerly Head of Department of Design & Technology, Dean of Faculty of Social Sciences & Humanities, Deputy Vice-Chancellor, Loughborough University. Researched and published in areas of design education: policy, curriculum, pedagogy, philosophy.

Niall Seery

Niall began his academic career in the Department of Education and Professional Studies at the University of Limerick in 2003 teaching on the first PGCE programme in technology education. He then joined the then Manufacturing and Operations Engineering Department where he took responsibility for teaching on the Concurrent undergraduate initial teacher education programmes (Materials and Engineering Technology Education and Materials and Construction Technology Education). Niall has taught Design and Communication Graphics, Process Technology and graphical and engineering pedagogics at both postgraduate and undergraduate level. In 2010 Niall established and is currently the director of the Technology Education Research Group (TERG) at the University of Limerick, which aims to advance technological education and support the continuous development of practitioners, initial teacher education, and second level pupils. Niall actively reviews for a number of international research conferences and is involved in a number of collaborative research projects. Niall has supervised a number of PhD and Masters students to completion, and is focused on developing the strategic direction of the TERG.

*9 7 8 1 9 0 9 6 7 1 0 3 4 *

An environmentally friendly book printed and bound in England by www.printondemand-worldwide.com

Reprint of # - C0 - 234/156/7 - PB - Lamination Matt - Printed on 05-Apr-18 23:51